THE
CLASSIC *f*M
PUZZLE
BOOK
365

First published in Great Britain in 2021 by Cassell,
an imprint of Octopus Publishing Group Ltd
Carmelite House, 50 Victoria Embankment
London EC4Y 0DZ
www.octopusbooks.co.uk

An Hachette UK Company
www.hachette.co.uk

All puzzles created by The Puzzle House, except puzzles 18, 26, 47, 58,
66, 87, 94, 96, 100, 139, 158, 170, 202, 323, 334, 342, 344, 352, 364 and
365 © Global Media & Entertainment Limited 2021

Classic FM is part of Global, the media & entertainment group.

ISBN 978 1 78840 338 2

A CIP catalogue record for this book is available from the British Library.

Printed and bound in the United Kingdom

1 3 5 7 9 10 8 6 4 2

Editorial Director: Joe Cottington
Editor: Ella Parsons
Deputy Art Director: Jaz Bahra
Designer: Jeremy Tilston
Assistant Production Manager: Allison Gonsalves
Product Management: Faye Leneghan, Joel Stern and Emma Neary

This FSC® label means that materials used for the product have been
responsibly sourced.

THE
CLASSIC *f*M
PUZZLE
BOOK
365

A CLASSICAL CONUNDRUM FOR EVERY DAY OF THE YEAR

FOREWORD BY
ALEXANDER ARMSTRONG

CONTENTS

FOREWORD

BY ALEXANDER ARMSTRONG

Welcome to another bumper book of classical music teasers, puzzlers, flummoxers and plain old hair-ripper-outers. This is the puzzle book for you if you have ever longed for there to be a version of Trivial Pursuit where all the cheese wedges were brown (apart from the *very* occasional pink one), or if the sound of Jeremy Paxman saying 'a music round now' brings on an almost scarily intoxicating endorphin rush.

In my year of presenting the Morning Show on Classic FM (Monday–Friday, 9am–noon, if you didn't know), I have come to recognize that mine is an audience with the sharpest minds, eyes and wits imaginable. One day we were discussing gardening gadgetry and a listener wrote in to tell me about the new leaf-blower they'd invested in, confessing that they rather loved it 'although I did once accidentally blow a chaffinch into a water feature'. Beat that.

In amongst all the tales of garden mishaps, East Anglian Scottish country dancing clubs, golf club green-keeping in County Down and anecdotes from the high altitude cab of a crane on the Bristol skyline (among many, many others – my listeners can be found anywhere and everywhere, if that doesn't sound too sinister. Or boastful...), I occasionally like to bang on a bit about the music I play, the composers responsible for the music I play, and indeed the musicians *playing* the music I play. I often wonder if anyone actually listens to all those juicy facts, or whether people simply prefer the *sound* of someone burbling gently about Finzi and are otherwise happy to let the nuts and bolts of the thing wash inoffensively over them like so much shampoo or other pleasing unguent.

Well, I need wonder no more because now is your (and indeed my) opportunity to put that to the test. From what I know about you, I reckon you'll have marked, learned and inwardly digested quite a lot. Particularly you, because *you* have bought this puzzle book and whoever heard of anyone buying a puzzle book if they didn't fancy their chances? In the same way I tend not to go and sit accountancy exams if I can help it, I suspect those who aren't of a fiercely competitive bent on all aspects of classical music will have given this book a cursory glance and moved on to another section of the bookshop – if they were even in a bookshop in the first place. Perhaps they mistook it for a Costa.

Anyway, I should very much like to know how you get on with the quizzes in this book. I almost feel as if it is a test of me as much as it is of you – so will you please get in touch and let me know?

Alexander Armstrong

PUZZLES

1 **NOTATION**

Each letter that appears in the treble clef (A, B, C, D, E, F and G) has been replaced by a musical note. The other letters of the alphabet are in place. Can you work out the name of the composer and a piece of their music?

♪ R I ♪ ♪

P ♪ ♪ R ♪ Y N T

2 **SPLIT PERSONALITY**

The letters in a composer's name have been split and rearranged. The composer's first name and surname both have four letters. The letters in each name remain in the correct order. Who is the composer?

J C A O G H E N

3 **NUMBER SUM**

Test your musical knowledge and your basic arithmetic skills in one puzzle.

Multiply the number of seconds in the nickname of Chopin's Waltz in D-flat by the number of corners on the hat in the name of the ballet by Falla.

4 **HALF TIME**

The clues below are listed at random, but they each have a four-letter answer. Solve the clues, then write the words into the grid so that the last two letters of one answer become the first two letters of the next. Each first letter appears in a numbered space.

1		2		3		4		5			

Clues

Man from *The Paradise Garden*?
Irish female singer
The first part of Stravinsky's bird?
The final word of a prayer
Study a score

5 **CYMBALISM**

Individual letters have been replaced by symbols. The first row names an instrument, the second a composer, the third another instrument and the fourth a theatrical cry!

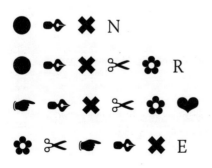

6 **METRONOME**

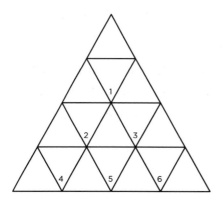

Each answer contains four letters. The first letter goes in a numbered triangle, the second letter directly above it, the third letter to the right and the fourth to the left.

Clues

1   Number in a quartet
2   Raised element on a stringed instrument
3   First chorus word of a 1740 patriotic song
4   German-born conductor Klemperer
5   Hit a drum
6   Anna's elder sister in Disney's *Frozen*

7 THREE DIVAS

Dido, Lulu and Mimi are three soprano soloists who are appearing together in concert.

All of them wear an evening dress, shoes and a wrap. Each woman wears a black item, a green item and a white item. The dresses, wraps and pairs of shoes are all of different colours.

Dido wears a black wrap, while Lulu sports white shoes.

What colours are the other items that the divas are wearing?

8 NUMBER NAMES

Each letter has been given a numerical value from 1 to 5. The total value of each word is reached by adding up the individual letters. No two letters have the same number.

D I V A = 10

A I D A = 13

A L D A = 16

What is the value of

V I V A L D I ?

9 OCTET

Solve the clues below to find the eight-letter answers. The first letter of the answer goes in the numbered square, and the answer can go clockwise or anticlockwise. You must work out which direction it goes.

Clues

1   Composer of the *Trout Quintet*
2   Romantic piece of music sung or played at a lady's window
3   Musical instrument, the prototype of the piano
4   Lead female character in *La Traviata*
5   Nationality of Aaron Copland
6   Programme of music planned and ready to be broadcast on radio
7   A note with half the time value of a minim
8   Gershwin's famous one was in blue

10 **HIDDEN INSTRUMENT**

Which musical instrument is hidden in the sentence below?
Discover it by joining words or parts of words together.

ALTHOUGH ASSOCIATED WITH CHURCH MUSIC,
PURCELL OFTEN WROTE FOR THE THEATRE.

11 **PHONOGRAPH**

Rearrange the letters to find the title of a long-established favourite
from the concert repertoire. There is one word in the title.

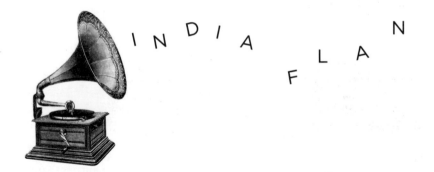

I N D I A   F L A N

12 **MISSING VOICES**

The voices are soprano, alto, tenor and bass. The letters S, A, T and
B (or some of these letters) are missing in the words below. Can you
identify the 'missing voice' letters to find the name of the work?

?HE ??R?ERED ?RIDE

13 SUDO-KEY

		C	mj					D
			mn		A			
E	mj				F			B
A					mj	D	G	E
mn					B		mj	
	F			A				
D	G				C			F
		mn	G					
			A		mn	G		mj

In this puzzle, each block of nine squares must contain the letters of the keys A, B, C, D, E, F and G, along with mj to denote a major key and mn to denote a minor key. Every row (going across) and every column (going down) must contain nine different keys.

14 **THE LOST CHORD**

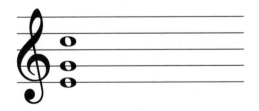

In a stave in the treble clef, the notes reading upwards in the spaces are F, A, C and E. The notes reading upwards on the lines are E, G, B, D and F. The sequence continues with notes above and below the stave.

Our stave shows a chord that has lost one note. The clue below leads to an answer made up of the letters of the notes shown in the stave, with an extra letter, A to G.

Can you find the missing note to complete the lost chord?

Clue
Composer and his pen?

15 **TYPO**

Someone has made a mistake when preparing the programme for a concert. It's only one wrong letter, but it creates a new word and gives the title of the piece a whole new meaning! From the clue, can you identify the well-known work as it appears in the programme?

Clue
This opera is about a noisy dog in an orange-growing area.

16 **WHAT AM I?**

My first is in BARS
But also in BEAT.
My second's in TEAM
But isn't in MEET.
My third is in RHYTHM
But isn't in RHYME.
My fourth is in MOTET
But isn't in TIME.
My fifth is in SING
And also in SOUND.
I am handy to have
When music's around.

17 **NOTATION**

Each letter that appears in the treble clef (A, B, C, D, E, F and G) has been replaced by a musical note. The other letters of the alphabet are in place. Can you work out the name of the composer and a piece of their music?

♪ R ♪ I N ♪ ♪ R

♪ R I ♪ ♪ ♪ ♪ I R

18 THE QUIZ FOR CLASSICAL MUSIC FANS

Put your music knowledge to the test with our truly tricky – and at times rather random – trivia quiz.

1 Name the animal that hit a cellist after falling off the stage during *Boris Godunov* at the Sydney Opera House.
a)   Cat
b)   Chicken
c)   Rabbit
d)   Dog

2 The number of keys on a standard piano is _____.
a)   86
b)   87
c)   88
d)   89

3 Tchaikovsky dedicated his famous overture to which year?
a)   1888
b)   1840
c)   1814
d)   1812

4 How many movements does Beethoven's Symphony No. 9 have?
a)   3
b)   4
c)   5
d)   6

5 What is the price of the most expensive opera costume of all time, worn by Adelina Patti in 1895?
a)   £2 million
b)   £15 million
c)   £61 million
d)   £174 million

19 **HEXACHORD**

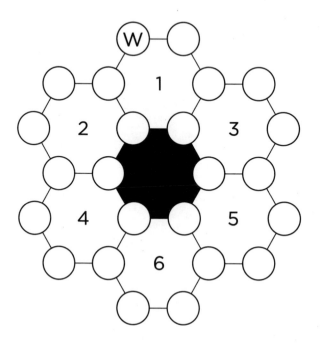

All answers have six letters. They can be written in the grid either clockwise or anticlockwise around the clue number. The first letter of Clue 1 is in place.

Clues

1   Polish city that is the subject of a famous concerto
2   The composer who wrote *Lohengrin* in 1850
3   Name given to perpetual canons for three or more voices
4   The section of the orchestra that violas belong to
5   If the interval between two notes is a whole tone, it is a major _ _ _ _ _ _
6   Sets of five parallel lines where notes are placed

20 **RING CYCLE**

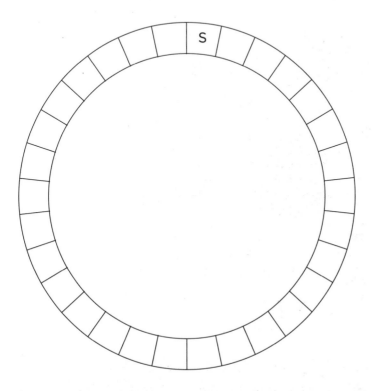

Solve the clues below, which are in no particular order, and slot the seven-letter answers into their correct places in the ring. The last letter of one answer forms the first letter of the next. Answer 1 begins with the letter S.

Clues

Small egg-shaped wind instrument
Patriotic hymns
Sir John, who wrote *The Crucifixion* in 1887
Music for a mass for the dead
A virtuoso

21 **SESTET**

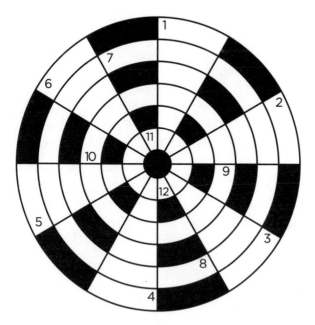

All answers have six letters. 1 to 6 start in the outer circle and are written towards the centre. 7 to 12 go around the rings in a clockwise direction.

Clues

1 First name of knighted conductor Davis
2 Surname of the prolific composer born Israel Baline
3 US-born Greek soprano Maria, famed for her dramatic roles
4 German poet whose work *Faust* inspired Gounod, Mahler and others
5 The refrains of a song come between the _ _ _ _ _ _
6 _ _ _ _ _ _ Bell – acclaimed violinist and conductor?
7 First name of Romanian soprano Miss Gheorghiu
8 Piece by Ravel used by Torvill and Dean in a perfect ice-dance routine
9 Instruments found in the woodwind section of the orchestra, which include piccolos
10 Name given to Beethoven's Ninth Symphony
11 Slightly discordant sounds of a plucked guitar
12 Profession of Cio-Cio San in *Madame Butterfly*

22 **INVISIBLES**

To solve this puzzle you need to use what you cannot see. Some letters of the alphabet do NOT appear in the box. Use each missing letter once to form the name of a composer.

23 **REARRANGEMENT**

There are two clues to help you find two solutions. The first clue leads you to a general word. The second clue leads you to a music-based word. You will need all your skills as an arranger, as the second word is an anagram of the first – it has all the same letters, but in a different order.

CHANGE AN AREA OF HABITATION BY SEASON

MUSIC POPULARISED BY SCOTT JOPLIN

24 **ADDERS**

Find two answers that can be added together to form a new word with a musical link.

What do you get if you add a metal container to something that is connected and working?

25 **VOWEL PLAY**

The name of a music venue is shown without its vowels. Can you identify it?

M T R P L T N P R H S

(Three words)

26 THE CLASSICAL MUSIC QUIZ DESIGNED FOR CHILDREN

Ready to put your school music knowledge to the test? Sure? It's your own time you're wasting...

1 What time period is Mexican composer Arturo Márquez from?
a)   Romantic
b)   20th century
c)   Renaissance

2 'Disjunct' is a smooth melody with no jumps. True or false?
True
False

3 Which of these instruments does *not* belong in the brass section of the orchestra?
a)   Tuba
b)   Trumpet
c)   Saxophone

4 Which note value is the longest?
a)   Breve
b)   Minim
c)   Dotted semibreve

5 Which minor key has four flats?
a)   C minor
b)   F minor
c)   A-flat minor

27 DIMINUENDO

Here are three clues to the identity of a famous composer. The number of points you earn diminishes the more clues you use. You earn THREE points if you only use Clue 1, TWO points if you need Clue 2, and just ONE point if you need Clue 3 as well.

Clue 1: A Czech composer, he was also an accomplished viola player.

Clue 2: His Symphony No. 9 was intended to celebrate the four hundredth anniversary of Columbus 'discovering' America.

Clue 3: His most famous opera is *Rusalka*.

28 **PRESTO**

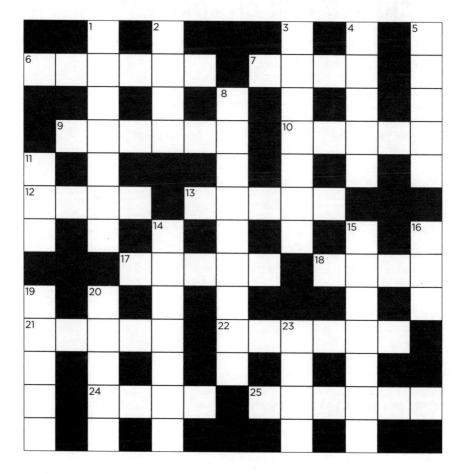

A classic quick crossword.

Across

6   Irish flautist James (6)
7   Latvian capital where Wagner had a post as musical director (4)
9   Describes the low-pitched recorder (6)
10 English conductor Sir Mark (5)
12 18th-century composer who wrote the oratorio *Judith* (4)
13 American folk musician Jay, composer of *Ashokan Farewell* (5)
17 Tchaikovsky's was *Pathétique* and Beethoven's was *Pastoral*. Which symphonies were they? (5)
18 A group of tenor and bass singers is a _ _ _ _ voice choir (4)
21 Home country of pianist Lang Lang (5)
22 London-born pianist Ms Cooper (6)
24 Seats in a theatre at the highest point (4)
25 Home of the second oldest of the five major American symphony orchestras (6)

Down

1   The high register of a trumpet (7)
2   Song from Handel's *Messiah*, 'Worthy is the _ _ _ _' (4)
3   Composer Debbie who set music to Alan Titchmarsh's poems in *The Glorious Garden* (7)
4   Austrian who wrote over one hundred symphonies (5)
5   A note that isn't natural or flat (5)
8   American conductor who often performed simultaneously as a soloist (9)
11 He became Master of the King's Music in 1942 (3)
14 Composer of *The Four Seasons* (7)
15 Argentine cellist Sol (7)
16 British conductor Gernon (3)
19 Surname of brothers Tom and Jonathan, keyboard players (5)
20 Writer of *The Watermill* (5)
23 Woodwind instrument (4)

29 **FIVE FIT**

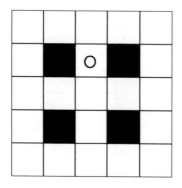

Solve the musical clues below, which are listed at random (all the answers contain five letters). Fit the answers into the grid, going either across or down. There is a starter letter to help you on your way.

Clues
Puccini opera
Rises very high in pitch
Musical sounds
Campanology is the study of them
Conductor's stick
Hungarian composer and pianist

30 **MUSIC BOX**

W	B	C	D	M	L
A	I	I	D	E	A
Q	B	T	D	E	R
A	B	C	H	A	T
A	O	C	E	E	Z
P	B	T	D	E	F

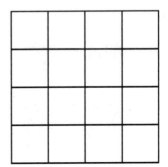

In a word square, the same words can be read either across or down. Your challenge is to make a word square in the empty grid. Three of the four words you need are hiding in the letter box, each one in a straight line that can go in any direction. The fourth word is the name of a musical instrument – you must decide which one!

31 **BACH-WORDS**

The name of a composer is hidden in the sentence below, but it has been written backwards. Look for a continuous line of letters from right to left to spell out the name.

HENRY IS ILL AT EASE PLAYING IN FRONT OF A LARGE AUDIENCE.

32 **SPIRAL**

1					2
		5			
4		8			
			6		
			7		
			3		

Solve the clues and write your answers in a clockwise direction in the spiral grid. Each answer begins in a numbered space. The words overlap each other in the spiral, with at least the last letter of one answer becoming the first letter of the next.

Clues

1   Ramin, who wrote the music for *Game of Thrones*
2   German composer who shares a surname with actress Marlene
3   Cuban dance, developed from the mambo (three words)
4   Pianist and conductor who established a Manchester orchestra
5   Yorkshire venue for a piano competition
6   John Williams film score, _____ *Years in Tibet*
7   Time of day when a serenade takes place
8   Parry's work, 'I Was _____'

33 **CIRCLES**

There are three circles and three words to be formed. The question mark stands for a mystery letter, which appears in all three words. Use all the letters in each circle once, including the mystery letter, to find the words.

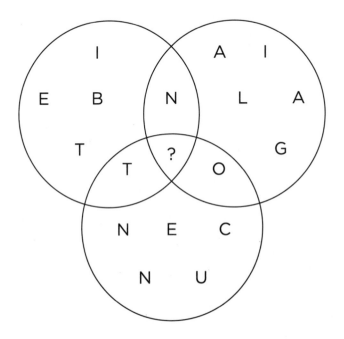

Clue
You are looking for the name of a composer and two of his pieces of music.

34 **COMPOSING**

Put the seven-letter words below in the grid in the right order to reveal the name of a famous composer in the diagonal shaded squares.

1						
2						
3						
4						
5						
6						
7						

BERLIOZ
CONCERT
COPLAND
ENCORED
POULENC
QUINTET
SALIERI

35 NAME CHECK

Look at the clues below, which are in no particular order. Write the answer to each clue horizontally in the grid. You need to work out the correct order so that the shaded columns reveal the first name and surname of a German composer.

1						
2						
3						
4						
5						
6						
7						

Clues

Scottish symbol and spiky plant
Little by little
Sunshade
The quality of not being boastful about your own achievements
Describes a sound that is not picked up
Short extract from a book or film
Groups of meaningful words

36 **NINTH SYMPHONY**

Each number from 1 to 9 represents a different letter of the alphabet. Solve the clues and write the letters in the correct spaces in the grid to reveal a music-related word or name.

1	2	3	4	5	6	7	8	9

Clues
a) Woodwind instrument   1299667
b) Song from an opera   2342
c) Sound on a scale   7658

37 **I WAS THERE**

Look at the world event below and the names of the three composers. Using your knowledge of when the composers lived, which of them could have said, 'I was there'?

THE FIRST FOOTBALL WORLD CUP, WHICH WAS WON BY URUGUAY

Gustav Holst
Leoš Janáček
Giacomo Puccini

38 TYPO

Someone has made a mistake when preparing the programme for a concert. It's only one wrong letter, but it creates a new word and gives the title of the piece a whole new meaning! From the clue, can you identify the well-known work as it appears in the programme?

Clue
An all-night illegal dance meeting takes place on an uninhabited Scottish isle.

39 BACK TRACK

There are two clues to help you find two solutions. The first clue leads you to a general word. The second clue leads you to a music-based word. The solutions are very similar, but in the second word the middle letter has moved *backwards* in the alphabet.

SHINY PAINT

AMERICAN COMPOSER OF *EINSTEIN ON THE BEACH*

40 **QUIZ CROSSWORD**

Work out the answer to each question in order to fill the grid.

Across

7 Which word completes the *Star Wars* title by John Williams, *The Phantom* _ _ _ _ _ _? (6)

9 Which piece in G minor is Albinoni most famous for? (6)

10 What name is given to the manager of an opera or concert company? (10)

11 In the initials CBSO, what does C stand for? (4)

12 Which German composer, first name Max, is widely know for his Violin Concerto in G minor? (5)

13 Whose *Canon and Gigue* is a popular piece of Baroque music? (9)

15 Who wrote *Madame Butterfly*? (7)

20 What completes the name of the operetta by Fraser-Simson, *The Maid of the* _ _ _ _ _ _ _ _ _? (9)

21 Which London hotel's name is linked to Gilbert and Sullivan operas? (5)

23 Who shares the title of the Purcell opera with Aeneas? (4)

24 What was Borodin's first and only complete opera? (6,4)

25 Which Jean-Philippe wrote *Castor and Pollux*? (6)

26 Which name completes the full name of the composer born in Broadstairs but who died in New York: Sir Richard _ _ _ _ _ _ Bennett? (6)

Down

1 In which country was Carl Nielsen born? (7)

2 What was Ravel's first name? (7)

3 What is the nationality of mezzo soprano Katherine Jenkins? (5)

4 Which instrument does Jess Gillam play? (9)

5 What was the first name of composer Arnold who wrote nine symphonies? (7)

6 In which decade of the twentieth century did Maurice Jarre win a Best Music Oscar for *Lawrence of Arabia*? (7)

8 Which work by Vaughan Williams was described as a romance for violin and small orchestra: *The* _ _ _ _ _ _ _ _ _ _ _ _ _? (4,9)

14 How is the Fairy described in *The Nutcracker*? (5,4)

16 The Gustavo Dudamel orchestra from Venezuela is named after which national hero? (7)

17 What name is given to repeat performances after requests from the audience? (7)

18 Which musical show, based on a Roald Dahl book, has music by Tim Minchin? (7)

19 Which word completes the name of the march used in the film *The Bridge on the River Kwai*: _ _ _ _ _ _ _ Bogey? (7)

22 What is a printed copy of a music composition called? (5)

41 **HALF TIME**

The clues below are listed at random, but they each have a four-letter answer. Solve the clues, then write the words into the grid so that the last two letters of one answer become the first two letters of the next. Each first letter appears in a numbered space.

1		2		3		4		5			

Clues

Work number to show the chronological order of a composition

Device on an organ that can be on or off

Ancient stringed instrument

Victorian ballad by Maybrick and Weatherley: *The _ _ _ _ City*

Musical notation sign to indicate a pause

42 **FAST FORWARD**

There are two clues to help you find two solutions. The first clue leads you to a general word. The second clue leads you to a music-based word. The solutions are very similar, but in the second word the middle letter has moved *forwards* in the alphabet.

A BATHROOM FITTING

COMPOSER

43 **RING CYCLE**

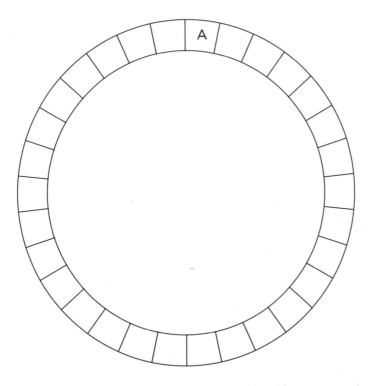

Solve the clues below, which are in no particular order, and slot the seven-letter answers into their correct places in the ring. The last letter of one answer forms the first letter of the next. Answer 1 begins with the letter A.

Clues

Walton opera, _ _ _ _ _ _ _ and Cressida
Series of eight notes
Name for an early English trombone
Czech composer of *Mà Vlàste*
First name of the 'red priest' Vivaldi

44 WHAT'S THE LINK?

Solve the clues below and write out your answers. What is the link between them?

Clues

1   Czech composer who wrote *The Cunning Little Vixen*
2   Holst's planet of war
3   Fantasy overture by Tchaikovsky, *Romeo and* _ _ _ _ _ _
4   A piano piece suggesting the night

45 ALPHA MALE

The letters below make up the name of a male singer, but they are presented in alphabetical order. Rearrange the letters to reveal the singer's identity.

A B E E F I L O

46 CYMBALISM

Individual letters have been replaced by symbols. The first row names an instrument, the second a female violinist, the third another instrument and the fourth a musical instruction.

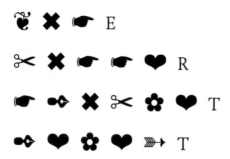

47 THE TRICKY MUSIC THEORY TEST

If you're looking for a quiz that you'll breeze through easily, close the book or turn the page now.

1 If a piece is marked 'Langsam', how would you play it?
a)   Slowly
b)   In the style of a march
c)   Delicately
d)   Energetically

2 Which period did Alessandro Scarlatti compose in?
a)   Romantic
b)   Classical
c)   Baroque
d)   Renaissance

3 How would you describe the time signature 12/8?
a)   Simple
b)   Complex
c)   Mixed
d)   Compound

4 If something is marked 'Smorzando', how would you play it?
a)   Solemnly
b)   Dying away
c)   Smoothly
d)   In a pastoral style

5 Which one of these Italian words is not a musical term?
a)   Squillo
b)   Verismo
c)   Pasticcio
d)   Crostini

48 MOVIE A TO Z

Here is the name of a movie with music that has featured in the Classic FM Hall of Fame – but the letters are shown in alphabetical order. Rearrange the letters to find a three-word movie title.

A C D E E H I L N O S S T V W W

49 PERFECT FIFTH

Solve the clues, which are listed at random. Each answer contains five letters. Complete the grid so that each answer starts in a space with an odd number and ends in the space with the even number that is one greater. To give you a perfect start, the letter in space 1 is A.

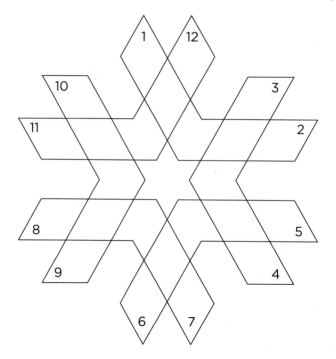

Clues

Measure for a series of notes
Collection, but not necessarily for stamps
Sounds like robbery from a Caribbean band
Follow this on a CD
Fruits from a famous tenor?
Composition with a sugary feel, we hear

50 MISS HERD

There is nothing Miss Herd likes more than listening in to other people's conversations. Unfortunately, she sometimes confuses words that sound the same but have different meanings. Can you help her out and correct the statement below? There are THREE words to change.

THERE IS AN ENORMOUS CUE AROUND THE OPERA HOUSE. THE BASE SINGER IS PROVING TO BE VERY POPULAR WITH HIS BANNED 'ENSEMBLE'.

51 FORTUNE TELLER

The fortune teller can see into the future. Whose fortune is she telling here?

'You will travel far from your homeland and find success in a country whose king is the same nationality as yourself.

The profits from the first performance of an oratorio in Dublin will be shared between two hospitals and a debtors' prison. This piece will become one of the most popular oratorios ever.

You will take part in a keyboard duel with your Neapolitan contemporary Domenico Scarlatti.'

52 JOHN WILLIAMS WORD SEARCH

```
P S E N O J A N A I D N I S X
H R C S D R A W A H S A T O J
A A E H T B A M P C R E S U H
N W C F I R E I O T Z K I N A
T R O R H N A N S M R L L D R
O A B O I N D E U A E M S T R
M T R C I U H L P R M T R R Y
M S R S C C I C E E M A E A P
E A T T R N I S R R U T L C O
N G O O C S O B M I S O D K T
A R R O S P A O A R I L N A T
C A L A M C V I N F C E I N E
E N R O M I A P O I T E H S R
O U C X E M N R R L E A C C T
J A W S H L Y R E M M Y S E R
```

Find the words linked to prolific film score composer John Williams hidden in the word square. All the words are in straight lines that run horizontally, vertically or diagonally. They may read forwards or backwards.

One film is listed twice – what is it? When Williams saw the film he said to its director, Steven Spielberg: 'You need a better composer than I am for this film.' Spielberg replied: 'I know, but they're all dead!'

AWARD
BAFTA
CINEMA
COMPOSER
CONDUCTOR
EMMY
FILM
GRAMMY
HARRY POTTER
INDIANA JONES
JAWS
JURASSIC PARK
LINCOLN
MOVIES
MUSIC
ORCHESTRA
OSCAR
PHANTOM MENACE
PIANIST
SCHINDLER'S LIST
SOUNDTRACK
STAR WARS
SUPERMAN
WAR HORSE

53 **OCTET**

Solve the clues below to find the eight-letter answers. The first letter of the answer goes in the numbered square, and the answer can go clockwise or anticlockwise. You must work out which direction it goes.

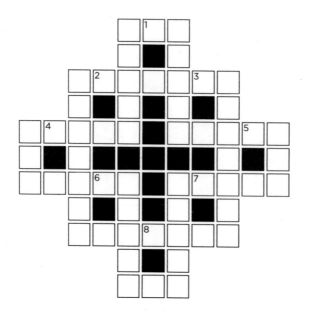

Clues

1 Elgar's song cycle *Sea* _ _ _ _ _ _ _ _
2 Brass instrument with a distinctive slide
3 Echoing
4 Words of an opera or oratorio
5 Piano piece suggestive of the quiet of night
6 French composer of *Manon*
7 Creator of the words of a song
8 Prolific film score writer John

54 THE LOST CHORD

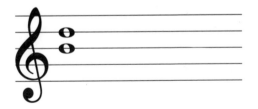

In a stave in the treble clef, the notes reading upwards in the spaces are F, A, C and E. The notes reading upwards on the lines are E, G, B, D and F. The sequence continues with notes above and below the stave.

Our stave shows a chord that has lost one note. The clue below leads to an answer made up of the letters of the notes shown in the stave, with an extra letter, A to G.

Can you find the missing note to complete the lost chord?

Clue
Description of an animal represented by a French horn when Peter was represented by strings?

55 NUMBER SUM

Test your musical knowledge and your basic arithmetic skills in one puzzle.

Shostakovich's Symphony No. 2 is dedicated to a month. His Symphony No. 3 names another month in its title. What number do you get if you add the number of days in each of these months together?

56 **METRONOME**

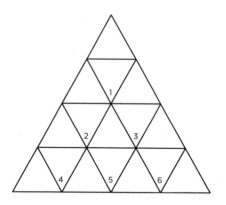

Each answer contains four letters. The first letter goes in a numbered triangle, the second letter directly above it, the third letter to the right and the fourth to the left.

Clues
1   Recipient of Rusalka's song
2   See clue 6
3   Italian lake much loved by Liszt
4   Sibelius's bird of Tuonela
5   The final part of a musical structure
6   'See, (6) the winter's (2)'

57 **VOWEL PLAY**

The name of a ballet is shown without its vowels. Can you identify it?

D P H N S N D C H L

(Three words)

58 THE QUIZ FOR MUSIC HISTORIANS

Think your general knowledge of classical music is a cut above the rest? You're going to love this quiz!

1 How many movements are there in Schubert's 'Unfinished' Symphony?
a)   1
b)   2
c)   3

2 Who wrote the piano piece nicknamed 'Rage Over a Lost Penny'?
a)   Scott Joplin
b)   Ludwig van Beethoven
c)   John Cage

3 How would you describe the long, continuous note that rises in pitch in the opening of Gershwin's *Rhapsody in Blue*?
a)   Con sordino
b)   Glissando
c)   Tremolo

4 Which composer was nicknamed 'The Little Mushroom'?
a)   J C Bach
b)   Schumann
c)   Schubert

5 Which composer is considered the 'father of the symphony'?
a)   Beethoven
b)   Haydn
c)   Mozart

59 WHAT AM I?

My first is in FIFTH
And also in THIRD.
My second's in DUET
But isn't in HEARD.
My third is in TENOR
But isn't in WROTE.
My fourth is in RECALL
And is also in NOTE.

60 **ENIGMA VARIATIONS**

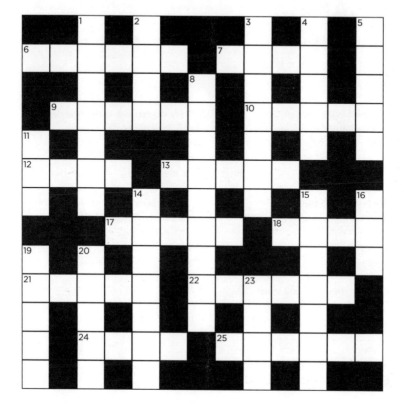

A cryptic crossword.

Across

6   Tug air and produce something strummed (6)
7   Game mixed-up in front of star; now a super star (4)
9   Unrest in Harlem, by innovative Bohemian (6)
10 Find Ian searching for home of sitar (5)
12 In the central steps, we hear, of massive continent (4)
13 One of our time in oratorio (5)
17 Composer of perfect joy (5)
18 Booty, it is said, with strings attached (4)
21 Numerical result of words and music (5)
22 Set down officially on disc (6)
24 Ram's star sign overturned? Holst found a different planet (4)
25 Hear the soundtrack here when iceman is rediscovered (6)

Down

1   Massive, memorable film music (7)
2   Lark on the move becomes *Armed Man* creator (4)
3   Barber, not Samuel, he hails from the home of oranges, not Florida (7)
4   Concealed, we hear, having written over 100 symphonies (5)
5   Not by Blake, but describes a harsh midwinter (5)
8   Horse and cart produce instrumental music (9)
11 Sponsors perhaps, to be Master of the King's Music (3)
14 Gore all thrown up a lively pace (7)
15 Squatter takes away first letter in some way to group of four (7)
16 Minor way of unlocking a door (3)
19 Palms upturned for religious song (5)
20 Roman revision for Bellini opera (5)
23 Cut small bit of film (4)

61 **QUICK QUOTE**

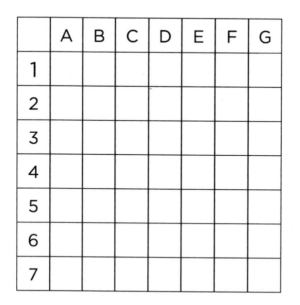

	A	B	C	D	E	F	G
1							
2							
3							
4							
5							
6							
7							

Solve the quick clues and write your answers across in the grid.

Clues

1   Elgar's occupation before he achieved fame as a composer
2   Elgar was writing for the festival in this Norfolk city when the *Enigma Variations* were successful
3   Elgar's middle name – the same as Walton's first
4   Along with melodies and harmonies, these make the third element of music
5   They are found in the string section, and Elgar played them
6   Compositions; the same word completes the titles _____ *de nuit* and _____ *de matin*
7   Home of Edward and Alice in Worcestershire, famous for its spa

Now, using the grid references (A1, B5, etc.), take the letter from the space indicated and write it below to reveal a quotation. This is from a line by Alice Elgar in Edward Elgar's *Sea Pictures*. Some would say it sums up the composer's thoughts.

C3.B2.D7.F1   C6.C7.C5.G6.B1   G4.G2.F3.D3.D5   E6.A1.B7.C4

_____   _____   _____   _____

62 **AS EASY AS ABC**

As easy as ABC ... or is it? Solve the quick clues, but remember that the letters A, B and C must be in each answer.

Clues

1   Prolific musical family whose members included August, Carl and many called Johann.

2   A native of the Auvergne, he wrote four volumes for voice and orchestra based on music from his native province.

3   A German composer and organist born in 1653, whose best-known work is a canon.

63 **PHONOGRAPH**

Rearrange the letters to find the title of a long-established favourite from the concert repertoire. There are two words in the title.

G O L I A T H

N O T

M A S O N

64 **HEXACHORD**

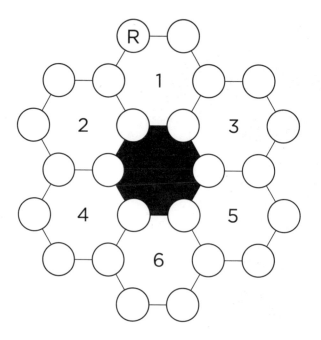

All answers have six letters. They can be written in the grid either clockwise or anticlockwise around the clue number. The first letter of Clue 1 is in place.

Clues

1   The country that is home to the Bolshoi Theatre
2   The country where Ketelby's Market can be found
3   The opposite of flats
4   The relationship that pianist Isata Kanneh-Mason has to cellist Sheku
5   German-born composer buried in Westminster Abbey in 1759
6   The word that begins the carol in English which starts 'Stille Nacht' in German

65 **SESTET**

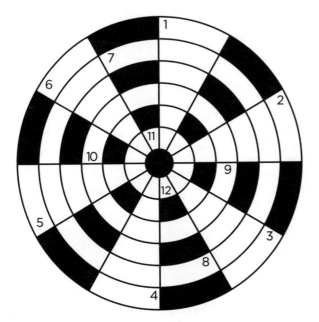

All answers have six letters. 1 to 6 start in the outer circle and are written towards the centre. 7 to 12 go around the rings in a clockwise direction.

Clues

1 Berlioz's first name
2 The Scott who popularised ragtime
3 Name given to the words of a song
4 Longer than a motif but shorter than a period
5 Where Carl Orff's opera *Prometheus* is set
6 The word that completes the name of the 'Coro di Zingari', from *Il Trovatore*: The *Anvil* _ _ _ _ _ _
7 Another name for a tune
8 Charlotte, who rose to fame as a classical singer with *Voice of an Angel*
9 The last part of a performance
10 The name that completes Humperdinck's famous work, *Hansel und* _ _ _ _ _ _ ?
11 Large music venues
12 In the title with Dido in the name of a Purcell opera

66 THE IMPOSSIBLE MUSIC TRIVIA QUIZ

Fancy yourself a music trivia expert? Put your knowledge to the test with this gruelling quiz.

1 Amy Beach is a significant woman in history because she was...
a) The first woman composer to win an Oscar for Best Score
b) The first English woman to compose and publish a hymn
c) The first American woman to compose and publish a symphony

2 How many children did J S Bach have?
a) 5
b) 13
c) 20

3 Which early 20th-century composer, born Philip Heseltine, had a heavy drinking problem and a penchant for black magic?
a) Carlo Gesualdo
b) Peter Warlock
c) Karlheinz Stockhausen

4 Who do we know as the first composer of polyphonic music?
a) Léonin
b) J S Bach
c) Bartolomeo Cristofori

5 If a piece is marked 'giacoso', how should you play it?
a) Very fast
b) In a mournful manner
c) In a fun, joyful manner

67 DIMINUENDO

Here are three clues to the identity of a famous composer. The number of points you earn diminishes the more clues you use. You earn THREE points if you only use Clue 1, TWO points if you need Clue 2, and just ONE point if you need Clue 3 as well.

Clue 1: Born in the USA, he started out as a song plugger on Tin Pan Alley.

Clue 2: In 1924, he wrote a piece as a concerto for piano and Paul Whiteman's jazz band. Toscanini, Stravinsky and Ravel attended the première.

Clue 3: He died in Hollywood aged 38, a few years after writing his 'American folk opera' *Porgy and Bess*.

68 **SUDO-KEY**

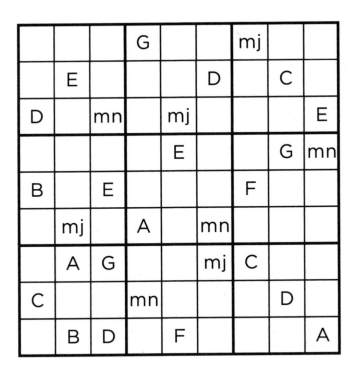

In this puzzle, each block of nine squares must contain the letters of the keys A, B, C, D, E, F and G, along with mj to denote a major key and mn to denote a minor key. Every row (going across) and every column (going down) must contain nine different keys.

69 **HIDDEN INSTRUMENT**

Which musical instrument is hidden in the sentence below?
Discover it by joining words or parts of words together.

THE OLYMPIC COLOURS WERE PARADED
AROUND THE STADIUM TO THE
ACCOMPANIMENT OF SOME STIRRING
MUSIC.

70 **NOTATION**

Each letter that appears in the treble clef (A, B, C, D, E, F and G) has
been replaced by a musical note. The other letters of the alphabet
are in place. Can you work out the name of the composer and a
piece of their music?

♪ ♪ ♪ H

M ♪ ♪ N I ♪ I ♪ ♪ T

71 **ALPHA MALE**

The letters below make up the name of a male singer, but they are
presented in alphabetical order. Rearrange the letters to reveal the
singer's identity.

A A B C E H I L L L M

72 **MUSIC BOX**

B	E	Z	D	M	T
P	O	Y	E	A	R
L	B	A	R	I	A
A	B	C	R	S	R
Y	U	S	Q	E	L
T	B	T	D	E	A

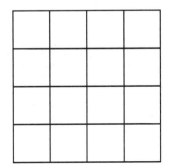

In a word square, the same words can be read either across or down. Your challenge is to make a word square in the empty grid. Three of the four words you need are hiding in the letter box, each one in a straight line that can go in any direction. The fourth word is the name of a musical instrument – you must decide which one!

73 **SPLIT PERSONALITY**

The letters in a composer's name have been split and rearranged. The composer's first name and surname both have five letters. The letters in each name remain in the correct order. Who is the composer?

F L R A E H N A Z R

74 **FIVE FIT**

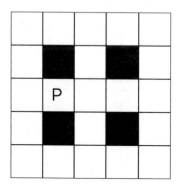

Solve the musical clues below, which are listed at random (all the answers contain five letters). Fit the answers into the grid, going either across or down. There is a starter letter to help you on your way.

Clues
Instrument in the string section
A voice, but not from the head
Low female voices
Musical play
The main performers in the above
A _____ score has words and music

75 **TYPO**

Someone has made a mistake when preparing the programme for a concert. It's only one wrong letter, but it creates a new word and gives the title of the piece a whole new meaning! From the clue, can you identify the well-known work as it appears in the programme?

Clue
Final selfie taken before autumn sets in.

76 **CIRCLES**

There are three circles and three words to be formed. The question mark stands for a mystery letter, which appears in all three words. Use all the letters in each circle once, including the mystery letter, to find the words.

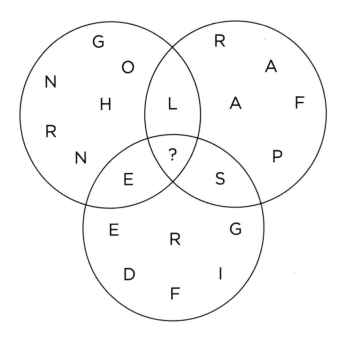

Clue
You are looking for three operas by the same composer.

77 SPIRAL

1				2	
				7	3
6					
	9				
5		8			
				4	

Solve the clues and write your answers in a clockwise direction in the spiral grid. Each answer begins in a numbered space. The words overlap each other in the spiral, with at least the last letter of one answer becoming the first letter of the next.

Clues

1 Patriotic hymn
2 Clarinettist Ms Johnson
3 Early song
4 Flautist James
5 Pianist Ms Wang
6 Polish composer and conductor Henryk
7 Leading opera and ballet company in the USSR
8 String instrument
9 Dido's song of mourning

78 NUMBER NAMES

Each letter has been given a numerical value from 1 to 5. The total value of each word is reached by adding up the individual letters. No two letters have the same number.

O D E = 6

R E E D = 8

R E C O R D = 19

What is the value of

R E C O R D E R ?

79 REARRANGEMENT

There are two clues to help you find two solutions. The first clue leads you to a general word. The second clue leads you to a music-based word. You will need all your skills as an arranger, as the second word is an anagram of the first – it has all the same letters, but in a different order.

BARRIERS THAT OPEN AND CLOSE

PERFORMANCE PLATFORM

80 **INVISIBLES**

To solve this puzzle you need to use what you cannot see. Some letters of the alphabet do NOT appear in the box. Use each missing letter once to form the name of a composer.

81 NAME CHECK

Look at the clues below, which are in no particular order. Write the answer to each clue horizontally in the grid. You need to work out the correct order so that the shaded columns reveal the first name and surname of a German composer.

1				
2				
3				
4				

Clues
Precipice
Stage performer
Pile of windblown snow
Convey from one place to another

82 FILLERS

Here are three words with the same letters missing. Find a single music-linked word to complete the longer words.

V _ _ _ _ T I O N S

P _ _ _ _ H

M A L _ _ _ _

83 **RING CYCLE**

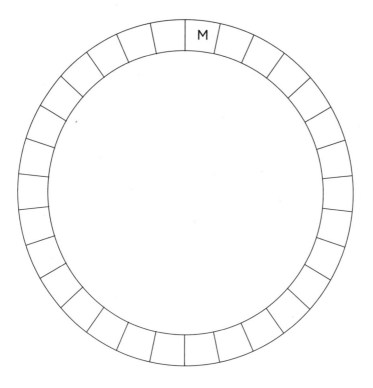

Solve the clues below, which are in no particular order, and slot the seven-letter answers into their correct places in the ring. The last letter of one answer forms the first letter of the next. Answer 1 begins with the letter M.

Clues
Pianist Murray who won the 1972 Leeds International Competition
Homage paid in a formal religious service
Arnold Schoenberg's country of birth
Regal is an _ _ _ _ _ _ _ of Elgar
Choral work by J S Bach, the *St* _ _ _ _ _ _ _ *Passion*

84 **FAST FORWARD**

There are two clues to help you find two solutions. The first clue leads you to a general word. The second clue leads you to a music-based word. The solutions are very similar, but in the second word the middle letter has moved *forwards* in the alphabet.

A PIECE OF LIFTING EQUIPMENT

COMPOSER

85 **BACH-WORDS**

The name of a composer is hidden in the sentence below, but it has been written backwards. Look for a continuous line of letters from right to left to spell out the name.

IT IS NOT LAWFUL TO PLAY MUSIC WHEN SOMEONE ELSE OWNS THE COPYRIGHT.

86 **I WAS THERE**

Look at the world event below and the names of the three composers. Using your knowledge of when the composers lived, which of them could have said, 'I was there'?

THE WORLD'S FIRST SUCCESSFUL HEART TRANSPLANT

George Gershwin
Percy Grainger
Igor Stravinsky

87 THE HARDEST EVER CHILDREN'S MUSIC QUIZ

You might be smarter than your music teacher when it comes to music theory know-how, but can you go back to basics and beat this quiz designed for children?

1 What is a tone poem?
a) A movement of music based on a poem or a verse
b) A piece of music in one movement, which paints an idea or theme
c) A sung piece of music, in spoken word style

2 What is the name of the section of a piece of music where a musician plays their instrument unaccompanied, with virtuosity?
a) Coda
b) Cadenza
c) Motif

3 By what nickname is Beethoven's Symphony No. 6 more commonly known?
a) Pathétique
b) Eroica
c) Pastoral

4 What is a musical palindrome?
a) A piece of music that endlessly repeats itself
b) Music where the key signature changes in every bar
c) Music that's the same when played backwards as it is when it's played forwards

5 Sergey Prokofiev wrote which famous musical composition for children?
a) *Peter and the Wolf*
b) *A Young Person's Guide to the Orchestra*
c) *Carnival of the Animals*

88 HALF TIME

The clues below are listed at random, but they each have a four-letter answer. Solve the clues, then write the words into the grid so that the last two letters of one answer become the first two letters of the next. Each first letter appears in a numbered space.

1		2		3		4		5			

Clues

Chopin prelude featured in the 1960s film *Taste of* _ _ _ _
Metrical foot used in poetry
In short, the top quality in reproduced sound
Long solo song from an opera
Area of Scotland and an instrument paired with the drum

89 NINTH SYMPHONY

Each number from 1 to 9 represents a different letter of the alphabet. Solve the clues and write the letters in the correct spaces in the grid to reveal a music-related word or name.

1	2	3	4	5	6	7	8	9

Clues

a) They appear with spaces on the stave   25679
b) Composer who married Robert Schumann 12343
c) French composer Erik   93857

90 **MOVIE A TO Z**

Here is the name of a movie with music that has featured in the Classic FM Hall of Fame – but the letters are shown in alphabetical order. Rearrange the letters to find a three-word movie title.

A A D D E E E I I L L N N R S V

91 **MUSICAL CONNECTIONS**

Make a connection between the words below by inserting the name of a musical instrument to finish one word or phrase and start the next.

1 KETTLE / _ _ _ _ / ROLL

2 BARREL / _ _ _ _ _ / GRINDER

3 TIN / _ _ _ _ _ _ _ / STOP

4 FRENCH / _ _ _ _ / PIPE

5 HAND / _ _ _ _ / JAR

92 **BACK TRACK**

There are two clues to help you find two solutions. The first clue leads you to a general word. The second clue leads you to a music-based word. The solutions are very similar, but in the second word the middle letter has moved *backwards* in the alphabet.

FRENCH NOVELIST WHO WROTE
THE THREE MUSKETEERS

COMPOSER OF *THE SORCERER'S APPRENTICE*

93 **REARRANGEMENT**

There are two clues to help you find two solutions. The first clue leads you to a general word. The second clue leads you to a music-based word. You will need all your skills as an arranger, as the second word is an anagram of the first – it has all the same letters, but in a different order.

DROVE BACK, REBUFFED

INTRODUCTORY PIECES OF MUSIC

94 THE MOST FIENDISH CLASSICAL MUSIC QUIZ EVER

If you can answer all these classical music questions, you're a genius. But no Googling – Mozart didn't use search engines in his exams and nor should you!

1 Which of these is *not* the subtitle of a Haydn symphony?
a)   Hornsignal
b)   Lamentatione
c)   Tragic
d)   Mercury

2 Which of Elgar's *Enigma Variations* was partially inspired by a bulldog?
a)   Variation XI (G.R.S.)
b)   Variation I (C.A.E.)
c)   Variation XII (B.G.N.)
d)   Variation IX (Nimrod)

3 Where was cellist Jacqueline du Pré born?
a)   Cheltenham
b)   Oxford
c)   Cambridge
d)   Cirencester

4 Which conductor always appeared on the podium wearing a white carnation?
a)   Sir Thomas Beecham
b)   Sir Malcolm Sargent
c)   Sir Henry Wood
d)   Sir John Barbirolli

5 How old was Giuseppe Verdi when he wrote his *Requiem*?
a)   50
b)   60
c)   70
d)   80

95 **PERFECT FIFTH**

Solve the clues, which are listed at random. Each answer contains five letters. Complete the grid so that each answer starts in a space with an odd number and ends in the space with the even number that is one greater. To give you a perfect start, the letter in space 1 is P.

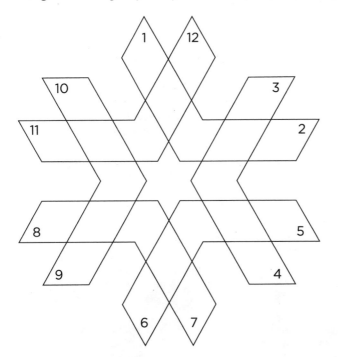

Clues

Thunderous applause
Sounds like animal feet in the break
Fruit significant for William Tell
Weapon called for in Jerusalem's second verse
Film award for lyricist Hammerstein
Goes on about stringed instruments

96 NAME THE CLASSICAL MASTERPIECE FROM THE EMOJIS

Are you a classical music buff? Can you speak fluent emoji? See if you can work out the name of the musical masterpiece from the emojis.

1

2

3

4

5

6

7

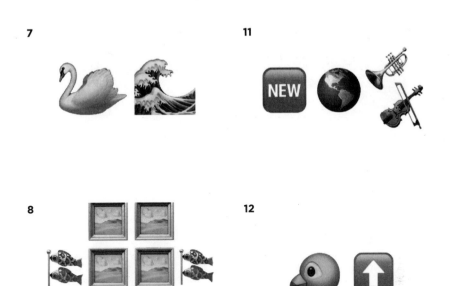

11

8

12

9

13

10

14

15

19

16

20

17

21

18

97 MISS HERD

There is nothing Miss Herd likes more than listening in to other people's conversations. Unfortunately, she sometimes confuses words that sound the same but have different meanings. Can you help her out and correct the statement below? There are THREE words to change.

THE ORCHESTRA PUT OUT A PLEA FOR A TENNER AS THEY WERE A SINGER SHORT. FORTUNATELY THE VIOLINIST COLLECTED HER MISLAID BEAU BEFORE THE PERFORMANCE BEGAN. WORRIED ABOUT THE PITCH OF HER INSTRUMENT, THE PIANIST WAS DESPERATELY TRYING TO LOCATE A TUNA.

98 FORTUNE TELLER

The fortune teller can see into the future. Whose fortune is she telling here?

'You will tour Scotland where you will meet the writer Sir Walter Scott.

'You will teach Prince Albert the piano.

'In 1843, you will establish a conservatory of music in Leipzig, assisted by Robert Schumann.

'You will become extremely popular in England, mainly due to the Victorians' love of the oratorio.'

99 QUIZ CROSSWORD

Work out the answer to each question in order to fill the grid.

Across

7   What was Handel's first name? (6)

9   Which instrumental music gets its name from the French for 'studies'? (6)

10   What was the first name of Spanish opera soprano Caballé? (10)

11   What is something listed in a programme called? (4)

12   Which Davis was an American trumpeter and composer? (5)

13   Which Verdi opera includes 'La donna è mobile'? (9)

15   A popular piece in a concert is known as a crowd what? (7)

20   What name, also used in ballet, refers to the melodic work of Schumann and Debussy (9)

21   Which voice does British opera star Freddie De Tommaso have? (5)

23   What is the name of the seamstress in *La bohème*? (4)

24   'Vesti la giubba' is from which Leoncavallo opera? (1,9)

25   Which Ms Graham choreographed Copland's *Appalachian Spring*? (6)

26   Which type of instrumental piece was given the title 'Moonlight' by its composer? (6)

Down

1   Which Spanish guitarist was born in Linares in 1893? (7)

2   Which composer co-founded the Aldeburgh Festival? (7)

3   What was the first name of composer Maxwell Davies? (5)

4   Who composed 26 Across? (9)

5   Which of Holst's *Planets* is the bringer of jollity? (7)

6   Which instrument like a small upright piano was patented in 1866? (7)

8   Which work did Carl Orff call his 'scenic cantata'? (7,6)

14   Which term refers to music that does not follow folk or popular traditions? (9)

16   Which word completes the piece by Handel, *The _ _ _ _ _ _ _ of the Queen of Sheba*? (7)

17   Which woodwind instrumentalists are not flautists or clarinettists? (7)

18   What was the first name of Welsh bass baritone Evans, noted for his operatic roles? (7)

19   What name is given to Widor's famous organ piece, often played at weddings? (7)

22   Which Sir Arthur was appointed Master of the Queen's Music in 1953? (5)

100 MATCH THE CLASSICAL COMPOSERS TO THEIR FIRST NAMES

Mozart, Bach, Beethoven... These great composers' names are familiar to us. But how often do we hear their *first* names? Match the composer to the correct name.

1 Let's start with Franz _____ Haydn. By which first name is this composer best known?
a) John
b) George
c) Joseph
d) Philip

2 How about the Russian giant, _____ Rachmaninov?
a) Andrey
b) Alexander
c) Maxim
d) Sergei

3 One of the first composers in the history of Western music: _____ of Bingen.
a) Hildegard
b) Gertrude
c) Evangeline
d) Belinda

4 Go on, we'll throw in an easy one here. _____ Amadeus Mozart?
a) Colin
b) Frideric
c) Wolfgang
d) Ludwig

5 Next up, dashing Italian Baroque composer Vivaldi – what was his first name?
a) Pietro
b) Antonio
c) Edoardo
d) Amedeo

6 What was the first name of Ragtime wonder, Mr Joplin?
a) Joe
b) Grant
c) Scott
d) Blake

7 Wagner wrote some of the greatest music of the 19th century. And his first name was...?
a) Robert
b) Roger
c) Roderick
d) Richard

8 Moving over to Austria now, and the great 20th-century composer, _____ Schoenberg.
a) Petroc
b) Arnold
c) Franz
d) Leon

9 And one final challenge. The name's Ravel. _____ Ravel.
a) Renaud
b) Thibault
c) Remy
d) Maurice

101 **CYMBALISM**

Individual letters have been replaced by symbols. The first row names an instrument, the second, third and fourth are composers.

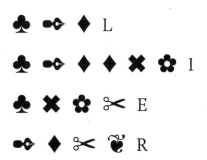

102 **VOWEL PLAY**

The name of a music venue is shown without its vowels. Can you identify it?

L S C L M L N

(Three words)

103 **THE LOST CHORD**

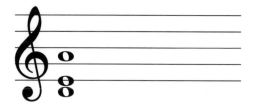

In a stave in the treble clef, the notes reading upwards in the spaces are F, A, C and E. The notes reading upwards on the lines are E, G, B, D and F. The sequence continues with notes above and below the stave.

Our stave shows a chord that has lost one note. The clue below leads to an answer made up of the letters of the notes shown in the stave, with an extra letter, A to G.

Can you find the missing note to complete the lost chord?

Clue
Isle providing the final destination for them in an early 20th-century symphonic poem?

104 **MISSING VOICES**

The voices are soprano, alto, tenor and bass. The letters S, A, T and B (or some of these letters) are missing in the words below. Can you identify the 'missing voice' letters to find the name of the work?

?? M???HEW P???ION

105 **COMPOSING**

Put the seven-letter words below in the grid in the right order to reveal the name of a famous composer in the diagonal shaded squares.

1						
2						
3						
4						
5						
6						
7						

DELIBES
GIBBONS
HARMONY
JENKINS
NATURAL
PHRASES
REPRISE

106 **SESTET**

All answers have six letters. 1 to 6 start in the outer circle and are written towards the centre. 7 to 12 go around the rings in a clockwise direction.

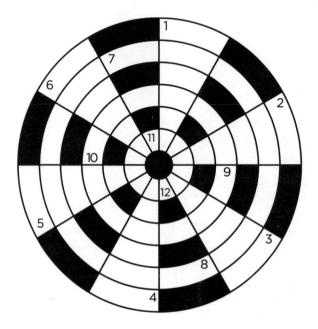

Clues

1   Caruso's first name
2   Acclaimed saxophonist Jess
3   Describing a combination of voices at the same pitch
4   French conductor with a famous father, Yan _ _ _ _ _ _ Tortelier
5   German region where J S Bach led Dresden's St Semper Opera
6   Official messenger who blows a trumpet to begin a proclamation
7   Nationality of composer and sitar player Ravi Shankar
8   Stately dance, popular in the sixteenth century
9   Hitchcock film, set in the Bates motel, with music by Bernard Herrmann
10 Conductor Barenboim's first name
11 Copland's work, *Fanfare for the* _ _ _ _ _ _ *Man*?
12 Word meaning 'performed' when referring to a musical instrument

107 OCTET

Solve the clues below to find the eight-letter answers. The first letter of the answer goes in the numbered square, and the answer can go clockwise or anticlockwise. You must work out which direction it goes.

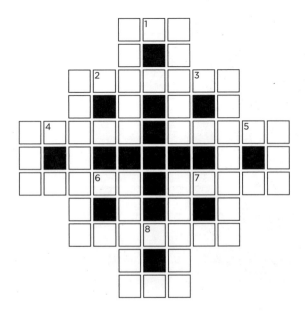

Clues

1   Composer of *Carmina Burana* (4,4)
2   Three-sided percussion instrument
3   Poetic and musical form dating from the 14th century
4   Piece of music with a rural, oral tradition (4,4)
5   A sacred musical piece such as Haydn's *The Creation*
6   An unnaturally high male voice
7   A note played in a detached way – the opposite of legato
8   Traditional Scottish musical instrument

108 **MUSIC BOX**

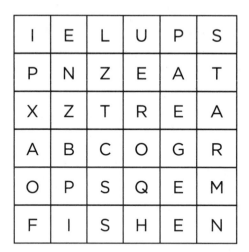
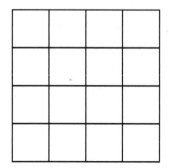

In a word square, the same words can be read either across or down. Your challenge is to make a word square in the empty grid. Three of the four words you need are hiding in the letter box, each one in a straight line that can go in any direction. The fourth word is the name of a musical instrument – you must decide which one!

109 **HIDDEN INSTRUMENT**

Which musical instrument is hidden in the sentence below? Discover it by joining words or parts of words together.

UNFORTUNATELY URSULA IS UNABLE TO PERFORM BECAUSE SHE CAUGHT FLU TERRIBLY BADLY.

110 **COMPETITIVE**

A college piano competition is down to four finalists. All four have performed and now have an agonising wait before the vote of the judges is revealed. The students are all good friends and can still enjoy some banter.

'There's no doubt that I'll finish first,' proclaims Viv. 'I reckon Will is going to be placed second, Tim third and Sally will be fourth.'

'You are so wrong,' laughs Tim. 'You won't be first, Viv, you'll be last! I'll get the first place, of course, with Sally second and Will third.'

'No way have I won,' says Will. 'Viv's going to be first, then Sally with Tim a close third and me well and truly last. What do you reckon, Sally?'

'Let's wait and see,' replies Sally.

As it turned out, Will was correct in one of his predictions. Neither Tim nor Viv had placed anyone in the right position.

In which position were the four musicians placed?

111 **NOTATION**

Each letter that appears in the treble clef (A, B, C, D, E, F and G) has been replaced by a musical note. The other letters of the alphabet are in place. Can you work out the name of the composer and a piece of their music?

♪ I N ♪♪

♪ L I Z ♪♪♪ T H ♪ N   S ♪ R ♪ N ♪♪♪

112 **FIVE FIT**

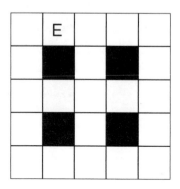

Solve the musical clues below, which are listed at random (all the answers contain five letters). Fit the answers into the grid, going either across or down. There is a starter letter to help you on your way.

Clues
Parts played in an opera
Orchestra founded in Manchester
Composer of *The Merry Widow*
Signs placed at the beginning of the staff
Song like, or relating to, the lyre
Signs that indicate no sound is made

113 **TYPO**

Someone has made a mistake when preparing the programme for a concert. It's only one wrong letter, but it creates a new word and gives the title of the piece a whole new meaning! From the clue, can you identify the well-known work as it appears in the programme?

Clue
Response from a bank when a failing pop duo want to cash in their assets.

114 **METRONOME**

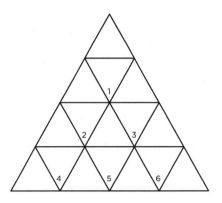

Each answer contains four letters. The first letter goes in a numbered triangle, the second letter directly above it, the third letter to the right and the fourth to the left.

Clues

1   Rachmaninov's work, *The _ _ _ _ of the Dead*
2   Tenor character in *Billy Budd*
3   A curved line indicating notes are grouped together
4   Dame Myra _ _ _ _, English pianist of the 20th century
5   Term to cover music, painting and theatre
6   A 1970s opera, *The Royal _ _ _ _ of the Sun*

115 **ADDERS**

Find two answers that can be added together to form a new word with a musical link.

What do you get if you add a keen follower to the cost of travelling?

116 **SUDO-KEY**

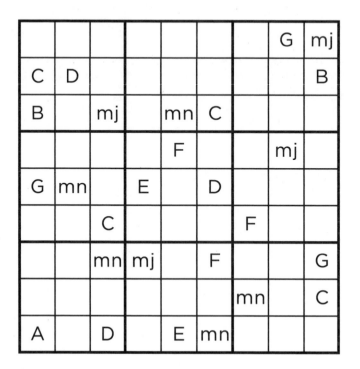

In this puzzle, each block of nine squares must contain the letters of the keys A, B, C, D, E, F and G, along with mj to denote a major key and mn to denote a minor key. Every row (going across) and every column (going down) must contain nine different keys.

117 **NUMBER SUM**

Test your musical knowledge and your basic arithmetic skills in one puzzle.

What number do you get if you add the digits that make up the year in the title of Tchaikovsky's famous Overture commemorating the defeat of Napoleon, and the number of Vivaldi's *Seasons*?

118 **SPLIT PERSONALITY**

The letters in a composer's name have been split and rearranged. The composer's first name and surname both have five letters. The letters in each name remain in the correct order. Who is the composer?

E T S H M Y E L T H

119 **PHONOGRAPH**

Rearrange the letters to find the title of a long-established favourite from the concert repertoire. There are three words in the title.

HER
SELFISH
PATER

120 **PRESTO**

A classic quick crossword.

Across

6 Pianist, composer and conductor André, who died in 2019 (6)

7 A piece for two performers (4)

9 Composer John who founded the Cambridge Singers (6)

10 Instrument played by Sheku Kanneh-Mason (5)

12 Actor Geoffrey who played David Helfgott in *Shine* (4)

13 Talent, great ability (5)

17 German tenor Kaufmann (5)

18 She meets Rodolfo in Act 1 of *La bohème* (4)

21 He was appointed Master of the Queen's Music in 1953 (5)

22 Location of Monteverdi's *Odysseus* (6)

24 Puccini opera, *The _ _ _ _ of the Golden West* (4)

25 Sponsor, supporter (6)

Down

1 French composer of *Pelléas et Mélisande* (7)

2 Film music by John Williams, played by Itzhak Perlman, *Schindler's _ _ _ _* (4)

3 17th-century composer who created *Dido and Aeneas* for a school (7)

4 Country of birth of Luciano Pavarotti (5)

5 Stick used by a conductor (5)

8 French composer of *Gymnopédies* (4,5)

11 Sailing vessel found in *Noye's Fludde* (3)

14 A small instrumental ensemble (7)

15 Lack of harmony of notes sounded together (7)

16 Lively dance (3)

19 Playwright who asked Grieg to produce music for his work *Peer Gynt* (5)

20 Song, 'Oh for the _ _ _ _ _ of a Dove' (5)

23 Beethoven, who was completely deaf, is reputed to have said, 'I shall _ _ _ _ in heaven' (4)

121 **LEADING LADIES WORD SEARCH**

```
E I N N E L G X R X M Z
J O H N S O N E Z N A Q
B B E E H A V N A N L N
B P E O S O A M I X L A
A E L N L X E L N V I M
T S A G E S U N S T G T
T M O M I D A W S O R R
E Y X W I M E U E W P O
B T X A U S A T A I O P
A H B H W F H N T Z R E
G U C H A R G E R I C H
G S V R E G N A L U O B
```

Find the names of women linked to the music world hidden in the word square. All the words are in straight lines that run horizontally, vertically or diagonally. They may read forwards or backwards. You are looking for the surname in capitals.

Marin ALSOP
Martha ARGERICH
Sally BEAMISH
Nicola BENEDETTI
Nadia BOULANGER
Isabelle FAUST
Sol GABETTA
Jess GILLAM
Evelyn GLENNIE
Jane GLOVER

Sofia GUBAIDULINA
Imogen HOLST
Emma JOHNSON
Rachel PORTMAN
Clara SCHUMANN
Ethel SMYTH
Yuja WANG
Judith WEIR
Debbie WISEMAN

122 **INVISIBLES**

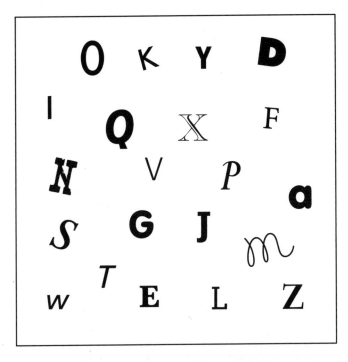

To solve this puzzle you need to use what you cannot see. Some letters of the alphabet do NOT appear in the box. Use each missing letter once to form the name of a composer.

123 WHAT AM I?

My first is in SPACE
But isn't in PLACE.
My second's in CHORD
And also in FACE.
My third's in ASCEND
And also in FALL.
My fourth is in LINE
And is also in ALL.
My fifth is in TUNE
And is also in GLEE.
Every good boy
Should know about me.

124 FILLERS

Here are three words with the same letters missing. Find a single music-linked word to complete the longer words.

_ _ _ I D I T Y

P O S T _ _ _ O U S

I N _ _ _ A N E

125 **RING CYCLE**

Solve the clues below, which are in no particular order, and slot the seven-letter answers into their correct places in the ring. The last letter of one answer forms the first letter of the next. Answer 1 begins with the letter C.

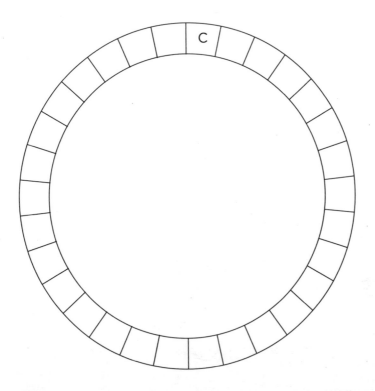

Clues

Composer of *Lakmé*

Brass instrument

1997 Oscar-winning film with music by James Horner

Person who is taught by a more experienced musician

Composer of *Fanfare for the Common Man*

126 **SPIRAL**

1					
		5			2
	7				
4			6		3

Solve the clues and write your answers in a clockwise direction in the spiral grid. Each answer begins in a numbered space. The words overlap each other in the spiral, with at least the last letter of one answer becoming the first letter of the next.

Clues

1 Composer of *Cavalleria Rusticana*
2 Beethoven's Choral Symphony is which in the sequence?
3 Rossini's magpie's crime
4 Venezuelan conductor Dudamel
5 Another name for a singer
6 Performance platform
7 Nationality of Robert Schumann

127 HALF TIME

The clues below are listed at random, but they each have a four-letter answer. Solve the clues, then write the words into the grid so that the last two letters of one answer become the first two letters of the next. Each first letter appears in a numbered space.

1		2		3		4		5			

Clues

Popular soprano Ms Upshaw
Magnetic recording and playback format from the 1960s
Nobleman from Gilbert and Sullivan's *Iolanthe*
Dear arrangement of a Wagner character?
Spanish dance

128 DIMINUENDO

Here are three clues to the identity of a famous composer. The number of points you earn diminishes the more clues you use. You earn THREE points if you only use Clue 1, TWO points if you need Clue 2, and just ONE point if you need Clue 3 as well.

Clue 1: This composer taught himself the cello and qualified in medicine.

Clue 2: He dedicated his 1880 'musical picture' *In the Steppes of Central Asia* to Liszt.

Clue 3: His opera *Prince Igor* was completed and partly orchestrated by Rimsky-Korsakov.

129 **CIRCLES**

There are three circles and three words to be formed. The question mark stands for a mystery letter, which appears in all three words. Use all the letters in each circle once, including the mystery letter, to find the words.

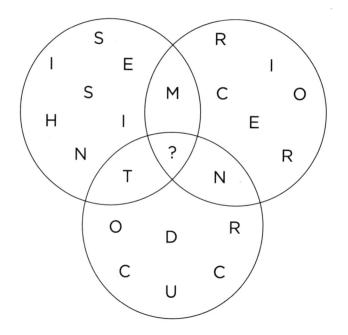

Clue

You are looking for a film score (two words), its composer and another musical role he undertook.

130 **NUMBER NAMES**

Each letter has been given a numerical value from 1 to 6. The total value of each word is reached by adding up the individual letters. No two letters have the same number.

S E T = 8

A C T = 11

O C T E T = 11

C O A T E S = 21

What is the value of

T O S C A ?

131 **BACH-WORDS**

The name of a composer is hidden in the sentence below, but it has been written backwards. Look for a continuous line of letters from right to left to spell out the name.

THE MILITARY BANDSMAN SAID REVEILLE WOULD BE PLAYED ON THE BUGLE THE NEXT MORNING.

132 **NAME CHECK**

Look at the clues below, which are in no particular order. Write the answer to each clue horizontally in the grid. You need to work out the correct order so that the shaded columns reveal the first name and surname of an Estonian composer.

1				
2				
3				
4				

Clues
Material elephant tusks are made from
Pleased, content
A ruby anniversary celebrates this number of years of marriage
Shatter, crack

133 **TYPO**

Someone has made a mistake when preparing the programme for a concert. It's only one wrong letter, but it creates a new word and gives the title of the piece a whole new meaning! From the clue, can you identify the well-known work as it appears in the programme?

Clue
This opera is about a man from Amsterdam who opens a fish and chip shop.

134 **I WAS THERE**

Look at the world event below and the names of the three composers. Using your knowledge of when the composers lived, which of them could have said, 'I was there'?

THE GREAT FIRE OF LONDON

Orlando Gibbons
Claudio Monteverdi
Henry Purcell

135 **MOVIE A TO Z**

Here is the name of a movie with music that has featured in the Classic FM Hall of Fame – but the letters are shown in alphabetical order. Rearrange the letters to find a two-word movie title.

A D E G G H I L M N N O O O R S T U

136 **NINTH SYMPHONY**

Each number from 1 to 9 represents a different letter of the alphabet. Solve the clues and write the letters in the correct spaces in the grid to reveal a music-related word or name.

1	2	3	4	5	6	7	8	9

Clues
a) Mezzo soprano Dame Janet   46127
b) Woodwind instruments   54529
c) Aria, 'One Fine _____'   863

137 **ENIGMA VARIATIONS**

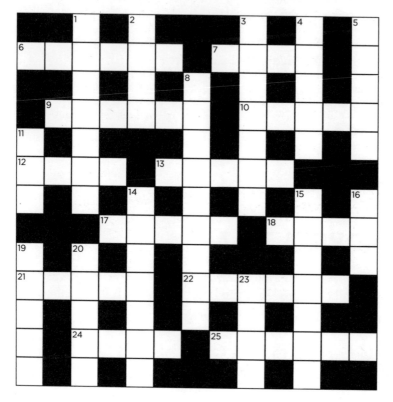

A cryptic crossword.

Across

6 A character in *A Midsummer Night's Dream* – not in Borneo! (6)
7 This Hunter has a simple melodious air by John Williams (4)
9 Short jacket favoured by Ravel (6)
10 Piano keys that were never ebony (5)
12 Air, a form of which is found in opera (4)
13 First name of singer whose surname suggests a weapon with a missile (5)
17 Rather splendid Bechstein? (5)
18 Courageous leader with her own entourage, apparently (4)
21 Um, taken away from the least possible and left with a note (5)
22 More the Parisian audience shouted! (6)
24 Liberated at the end of line two in 'Land of Hope and Glory' (4)
25 Evince a change of route for the gondoliers (6)

Down

1 Guitarist goes via a diversion (7)
2 Was this string quartet a prank by Haydn? (4)
3 A saintly patroness of music (7)
4 Missile associate with 13 Across, and Tell? (5)
5 Makes music from an instrument and dramas (5)
8 One of two musical French sisters, adept at bread-making? (9)
11 Wicked with the Good and the Ugly (3)
14 Brass instrument found in a daffodil (7)
15 Desist from the chorus (7)
16 Owl produces note, not a high one (3)
19 Dame Nellie got confused on leisurely walk (5)
20 Mac's weapon in opera for the destitute (5)
23 Seen with the staff who have lots of lines (4)

138 PERFECT FIFTH

Solve the clues, which are listed at random. Each answer contains five letters. Complete the grid so that each answer starts in a space with an odd number and ends in the space with the even number that is one greater. To give you a perfect start, the letter in space 1 is T.

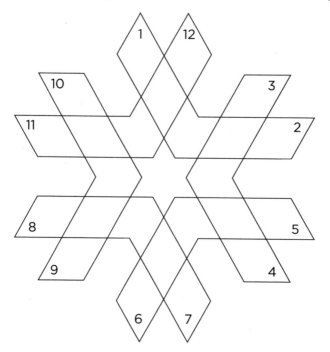

Clues

Major spouse in opera?
Puts an end to organ controls
Cunning little Janáček opera
Take pains to find Domingo's birthplace
Female composer lacking vowels
Banknote, we hear for a singer

139 'ODE TO JOY' OR THE US CONSTITUTION?

The Constitution of the United States was penned in 1787 by George Washington and his Founding Father chums. Just one year earlier, Friedrich Schiller wrote his poem 'Ode to Joy', which Beethoven set to music in the climatic finale to his Ninth Symphony. Both works, in very different ways, articulate ideals of freedom and liberty, one in a legal and political text, the other in poetry. But can you tell them apart?

1 'All people become brothers'
a)   Ode to Joy
b)   US Constitution

2 'We the People'
a)   Ode to Joy
b)   US Constitution

3 'Be embraced, Millions'
a)   Ode to Joy
b)   US Constitution

4 'To be a friend's friend'
a)   Ode to Joy
b)   US Constitution

5 'Giving them aid and comfort'
a)   Ode to Joy
b)   US Constitution

6 'Whoever has succeeded in the great attempt'
a)   Ode to Joy
b)   US Constitution

7 'A more perfect union'
a)   Ode to Joy
b)   US Constitution

8 'He shall from time to time'
a)   Ode to Joy
b)   US Constitution

9 'We have hereunto subscribed'
a)   Ode to Joy
b)   US Constitution

140 **ALPHA MALE**

The letters below make up the name of a male singer, but they are presented in alphabetical order. Rearrange the letters to reveal the singer's identity.

A A B C D E E I L L N O R

141 **FORTUNE TELLER**

The fortune teller can see into the future. Whose fortune is she telling here?

'George Bernard Shaw will proclaim that you are the rightful heir to Verdi.

'One of your operas will be used as the basis for a musical, moving the setting from one Asian country to another.

'One of your arias will be used as an anthem at a worldwide sporting event.'

142 **MISSING VOICES**

The voices are soprano, alto, tenor and bass. The letters S, A, T and B (or some of these letters) are missing in the words below. Can you identify the 'missing voice' letters to find the name of the work?

C O ? Ì   F ? N   ? U ? ? E

143 **MUSIC BOX**

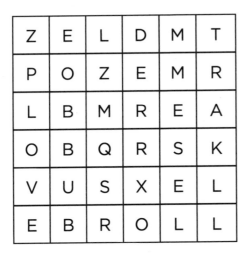
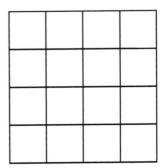

In a word square, the same words can be read either across or down. Your challenge is to make a word square in the empty grid. Three of the four words you need are hiding in the letter box, each one in a straight line that can go in any direction. The fourth word is the name of a musical instrument – you must decide which one!

144 **MUSICAL MENU**

DAD enjoys visiting the CAFE for a spot of lunch. If he fancies something hot, his favourite is BEEF with a generous portion of CABBAGE. If it's a warm day, or if he's in a hurry, he opts for a sandwich. Does he go for EGG or CHEESE?.

145 **BACK TRACK**

There are two clues to help you find two solutions. The first clue leads you to a general word. The second clue leads you to a music-based word. The solutions are very similar, but in the second word the middle letter has moved *backwards* in the alphabet.

TRADITIONAL COUNTRY OR CHRISTMAS EVENT WHERE GOODS ARE BOUGHT AND SOLD

FRENCH COMPOSER OF A FAMOUS *REQUIEM*

146 **FAST FORWARD**

There are two clues to help you find two solutions. The first clue leads you to a general word. The second clue leads you to a music-based word. The solutions are very similar, but in the second word the middle letter has moved *forwards* in the alphabet.

TOMBS

ENGLISH CONDUCTOR

147 **QUICK QUOTE**

	A	B	C	D	E	F	G
1							
2							
3							
4							
5							
6				▓			
7							

Solve the quick clues and write your answers across in the grid.

Clues

1   Country where Menuhin was born
2   Nationality he took in 1985
3   City where he became an overnight celebrity at the age of 11 (3,4)
4   Concluding parts of performances
5   To direct, which he did after founding his own chamber orchestra
6   It draws the sound from the strings (3) / A group of two, like Menuhin and Grappelli (3)
7   His autobiography was *Unfinished* _ _ _ _ _ _ _

Now, using the grid references (A1, B5, etc.), take the letter from the space indicated and write it below to reveal a quotation. This is a quote from Yehudi Menuhin, which completes one of his definitions of music.

F1.B2.B3.G1.G5.F7.F2   B6.D1. E6.C1.F3   E3.E5.D2   G6.A4

_____   _____   ____   ____

A5.G2.A1.B5.G4

_____

148 **METRONOME**

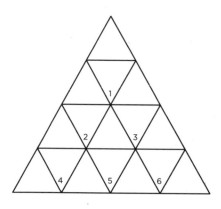

Each answer contains four letters. The first letter goes in a numbered triangle, the second letter directly above it, the third letter to the right and the fourth to the left.

Clues

1   Singer Michael who often duets with Alfie Boe
2   Unaccompanied song
3   2019 Harlem-based opera about protestors and the police
4   Bernstein classic, _ _ _ _ *Side Story*
5   Musical scales
6   Gilbert and Sullivan's courtroom caper, *Trial by* _ _ _ _

149 **NUMBER SUM**

Test your musical knowledge and your basic arithmetic skills in one puzzle.

What number do you get if you multiply the number of Strauss's *Last Songs*, by the number of *Years in Tibet* in John Williams' movie soundtrack?

150 SESTET

All answers have six letters. 1 to 6 start in the outer circle and are written towards the centre. 7 to 12 go around the rings in a clockwise direction.

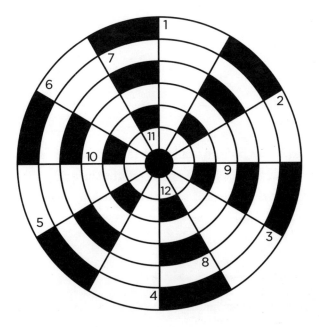

Clues

1 Gustav, born in Bohemia in 1860
2 Miss Norman, who made her La Scala debut in 1972
3 Prokofiev ballet which, when first presented to the Bolshoi, was deemed un-danceable: *Romeo and* _ _ _ _ _ _
4 Short musical advertising theme
5 Name given to a particular gift or aptitude
6 He had a father called Leopold and a wife called Constanze
7 French composer who played the organ and harpsichord, and whose first opera was *Hippolyte et Aricie*
8 It follows *The* in the title of Gilbert and Sullivan's opera set in Japan
9 Gramophone record with just one piece of music on each side of the disc
10 Vaughan Williams used a memorable 'Fantasia on a Theme by' composer Thomas
11 Profession that Vivaldi trained in
12 A group of seven musicians

151 **FIVE FIT**

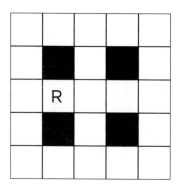

Solve the musical clues below, which are listed at random (all the answers contain five letters). Fit the answers into the grid, going either across or down. There is a starter letter to help you on your way.

Clues
Ensemble or band
Roles assigned to performers in an opera or operetta
British composer of a famous cello concerto in 1919
Conductor who is not the regular wielder of the baton at a performance
Sounds, which have particular pitch and quality
Musical instrument found in a church

152 **HIDDEN INSTRUMENT**

Which musical instrument is hidden in the sentence below? Discover it by joining words or parts of words together.

HENRY HEARD RUMOURS THAT A BRAND NEW COMPOSITION WAS TO BE PREMIERED THAT VERY EVENING.

153 **THE LOST CHORD**

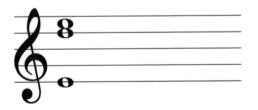

In a stave in the treble clef, the notes reading upwards in the spaces are F, A, C and E. The notes reading upwards on the lines are E, G, B, D and F. The sequence continues with notes above and below the stave.

Our stave shows a chord that has lost one note. The clue below leads to an answer made up of the letters of the notes shown in the stave, with an extra letter, A to G.

Can you find the missing note to complete the lost chord?

Clue
What to do with birds on the steps of St Paul's Cathedral?

154 **CYMBALISM**

Individual letters have been replaced by symbols. The first row names an instrument, the second an English pianist, the third a composer and the fourth another composer.

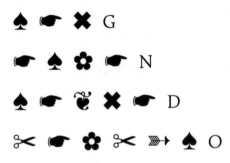

155 **SPIRAL**

1			2		
				6	
		8			
					3
5			7		
	4				

Solve the clues and write your answers in a clockwise direction in the spiral grid. Each answer begins in a numbered space. The words overlap each other in the spiral, with at least the last letter of one answer becoming the first letter of the next.

Clues

1 Paul, composer of the *Victorian Kitchen Garden Suite*
2 Creator of *Lakmé*
3 Home country of Veljo Tormis
4 Verdi chorus
5 Brazilian composer (two words)
6 Home of a Massachusetts symphony orchestra
7 Opera, *Eugene* _____
8 'Handle' of a guitar or violin

156 **CIRCLES**

There are three circles and three words to be formed. The question mark stands for a mystery letter, which appears in all three words. Use all the letters in each circle once, including the mystery letter, to find the words.

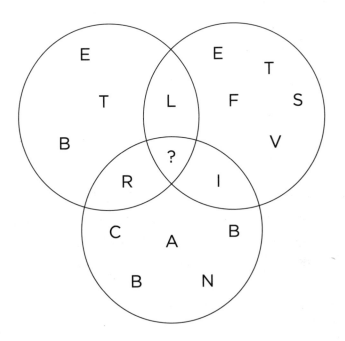

Clue
You are looking for three concert halls.

157 **OCTET**

Solve the clues below to find the eight-letter answers. The first
letter of the answer goes in the numbered square, and the answer
can go clockwise or anticlockwise. You must work out which
direction it goes.

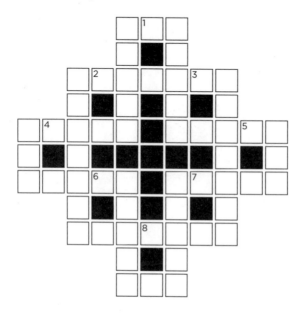

Clues

1   Creator of a musical work
2   Lyric compositions with French words (and the French word for songs)
3   Appreciative clapping
4   A group of players or singers
5   Groups of five performers
6   This American wrote *The Seal Lullaby*
7   Clara, who was the focus of the album *Romance* by Isata Kanneh-Mason
8   Puccini's final opera, which he didn't complete himself

158 **OPERA OR APPLE?**

They say an apple a day keeps the doctor away – but do you know your Doktor Faustus from your Royal Gala? Your pommes from your pêcheurs de perles? If you think you know your opera to the core, we challenge you to this juicy quiz. For each one, say whether it is an opera or an apple!

1	Reinette du Canada	13	Fierrabras
2	Golden Delicious	14	Golden Cockerel
3	King Priam	15	Gerheimrat Dr Oldenburg
4	Tydeman's Late Orange	16	Liberty
5	Boris Godunov	17	The Beauty of Bath
6	St Edmund's Pippin	18	Un Giorno di Regno
7	Merry Widow	19	Esopus Spitzenburg
8	Lucia di Lammermoor	20	Roxbury Russet
9	Jonagold	21	Cavalleria Rusticana
10	Melba	22	Belleza de Roma
11	Armida	23	Idared
12	Birgit Bonnier		

159 **VOWEL PLAY**

The name of a ballet is shown without its vowels. Can you identify it?

B T Y N D T H B S T

(Four words)

160 **PERFECT FIFTH**

Solve the clues, which are listed at random. Each answer contains five letters. Complete the grid so that each answer starts in a space with an odd number and ends in the space with the even number that is one greater. To give you a perfect start, the letter in space 1 is S.

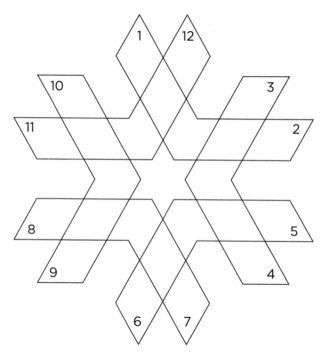

Clues
Tides change musical revisions
Overturn riots in groups of three
Helpers needed to play the keyboard
Take a letter away from the melody sung in the mountains
Jump at the beginning of a concert
Sell small items, we hear, on the piano

161 **INVISIBLES**

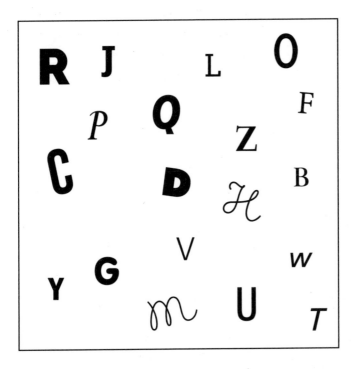

To solve this puzzle you need to use what you cannot see. Some letters of the alphabet do NOT appear in the box. Use each missing letter once to form the name of a composer.

162 **ADDERS**

Find two answers that can be added together to form a new word with a musical link.

What do you get if you add a scam to a sure-fire winner?

163 HALF TIME

The clues below are listed at random, but they each have a four-letter answer. Solve the clues, then write the words into the grid so that the last two letters of one answer become the first two letters of the next. Each first letter appears in a numbered space.

1		2		3		4		5			

Clues

Move at speed with the Valkyries

Tom Hiddleston's super-villain character in *Avengers Assemble,* with a Schubert backing

Trade in musical memorabilia or gain a recording contract

Welsh singer and presenter Mr Jones

Dame _ _ _ Te Kanawa

164 NOTATION

Each letter that appears in the treble clef (A, B, C, D, E, F and G) has been replaced by a musical note. The other letters of the alphabet are in place. Can you work out the name of the composer and a piece of their music?

♪ I N ♪ U ♪ I

L ♪ O N ♪ ♪

165 SUDO-KEY

	E			D				
G					C	mj	F	E
		mj	G				A	
	F						G	
		C		E	A			
mj				G		E		D
A						mn		B
B	mn		C				E	
		F	mj		B			

In this puzzle, each block of nine squares must contain the letters of the keys A, B, C, D, E, F and G, along with mj to denote a major key and mn to denote a minor key. Every row (going across) and every column (going down) must contain nine different keys.

166 **REARRANGEMENT**

There are two clues to help you find two solutions. The first clue leads you to a general word. The second clue leads you to a music-based word. You will need all your skills as an arranger, as the second word is an anagram of the first – it has all the same letters, but in a different order.

RULES AS A MONARCH

VOCALIST

167 **DIMINUENDO**

Here are three clues to the identity of a famous composer. The number of points you earn diminishes the more clues you use. You earn THREE points if you only use Clue 1, TWO points if you need Clue 2, and just ONE point if you need Clue 3 as well.

Clue 1: This Yorkshire-born composer was lent money by his father to open an orange plantation in Florida.

Clue 2: He settled in Paris, adopting a Bohemian lifestyle and making friends with Strindberg and Gauguin.

Clue 3: In the early 1920s he became blind, and his works were noted by Eric Fenby.

168 **SALE PRICE**

A shopkeeper buys an antique cello, which she puts in to her shop of musical collectables. She adds 25% to the price that she paid. Unfortunately, the cello attracts little interest and sits collecting dust in the shop.

In the accepted bartering techniques of TV antique shows, someone makes a cheeky offer and asks for 50% off the ticket price.

The shopkeeper is happy to free up the space by selling the cello and agrees a price that meets in the middle, and is 25% off the ticket price.

The shopkeeper paid £2,000 for the cello.

How much did she sell it for?

169 **PHONOGRAPH**

Rearrange the letters to find the title of a long-established favourite from the concert repertoire. There are three words in the title.

CHEF

MEAT

GUILT

170 A CLASSICAL MUSIC GENERAL KNOWLEDGE CHALLENGE

Hone your quizzing abilities with this general knowledge challenge. If you can get all the questions right, you can truly claim to be a classical music expert!

1 Which of these actors has *not* played Beethoven on screen?
a) John Belushi
b) Gary Oldman
c) Ed Harris
d) Simon Callow

2 In Purcell's *Dido and Aeneas*, where is Dido queen of?
a) Carthage
b) Egypt
c) Troy
d) Rome

3 In which year did the Sydney Opera House open?
a) 1971
b) 1972
c) 1973
d) 1974

4 Which of these composers was given the title of Master of the Queen's Music?
a) W S Gilbert
b) Sir Walter Parratt
c) Frank Bridge
d) Harold Darke

5 Which of these artists did *not* perform with Luciano Pavarotti during his lifetime?
a) Sheryl Crow
b) Celine Dion
c) The Spice Girls
d) Madonna

171 **NINTH SYMPHONY**

Each number from 1 to 9 represents a different letter of the alphabet. Solve the clues and write the letters in the correct spaces in the grid to reveal a music-related word or name.

1	2	3	4	5	6	7	8	9

Clues

a) Groups of singers   815739
b) A note worth two crotchets   47674
c) Piece of military music   42381

172 **NUMBER NAMES**

Each letter has been given a numerical value from 1 to 6. The total value of each word is reached by adding up the individual letters. No two letters have the same number.

N O T E = 10

T E N O R = 15

E N T E R = 18

C O R N E T = 21

What is the value of

R O C O C O ?

127

173 **SPLIT PERSONALITY**

The letters in a composer's name have been split and rearranged. The composer's first name and surname both have five letters. The letters in each name remain in the correct order. Who is the composer?

F L R I A S Z N Z T

174 **FILLERS**

Here are three words with the same letters missing. Find a single music-linked word to complete the longer words.

N O N _ _ _ _ E N C E

R A _ _ _ _ I

_ _ _ _ E T S

175 **BACH-WORDS**

The name of a composer is hidden in the sentence below, but it has been written backwards. Look for a continuous line of letters from right to left to spell out the name.

HE CAN'T TELL A TREBLE CLEF FROM A BASS CLEF, NEVER MIND PLAYING THE PIECE OF MUSIC!

176 HEXACHORD

All answers have six letters. They can be written in the grid either clockwise or anticlockwise around the clue number. The first letter of Clue I is in place.

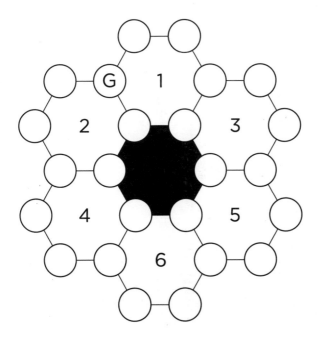

Clues

1   Composer Edward _ _ _ _ _ _ who (confusingly) wrote *Merrie England*
2   Word that completes the Stravinsky ballet, *The Rite of* _ _ _ _ _ _
3   The *Variations* that are amongst Elgar's most popular works
4   Title of the movie whose music was written by John Barry: *Out of* _ _ _ _ _ _
5   A student does this on putting their name down for a course
6   Surname of virtuoso cellist Pablo

177 **NAME CHECK**

Look at the clues below, which are in no particular order. Write the answer to each clue horizontally in the grid. You need to work out the correct order so that the shaded columns reveal the first name and surname of an American composer.

1				
2				
3				
4				
5				
6				

Clues
Each, all
Representative
Slow-moving creature
Name of a book or film
Arms and legs
Wept or shouted

178 **RING CYCLE**

Solve the clues below, which are in no particular order, and slot the seven-letter answers into their correct places in the ring. The last letter of one answer forms the first letter of the next. Answer 1 begins with the letter E.

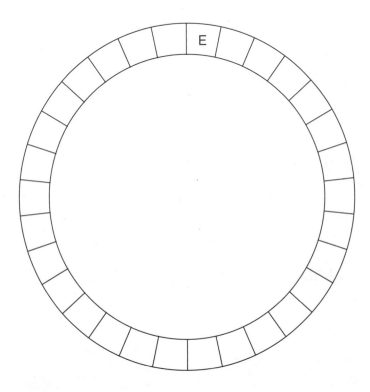

Clues

Music instruction which means 'at a walking pace'
Pianist and composer of *I Giorni*
A note that is neither flat nor sharp
Two-act opera by Ferdinando Paer
Nationality of two musicians in two other answers

179 **FAST FORWARD**

There are two clues to help you find two solutions. The first clue leads you to a general word. The second clue leads you to a music-based word. The solutions are very similar, but in the second word the middle letter has moved *forwards* in the alphabet.

GREEN LEAFY VEGETABLE

THREE OR MORE NOTES SOUNDED SIMULTANEOUSLY

180 **I WAS THERE**

Look at the world event below and the names of the three composers. Using your knowledge of when the composers lived, which of them could have said, 'I was there'?

THE FIRST MODERN OLYMPICS TOOK PLACE IN ATHENS

Alexander Borodin
Johannes Brahms
Pyotr Ilyich Tchaikovsky

181 FIVE FIT

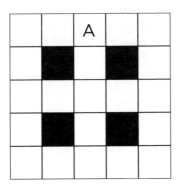

Solve the musical clues below, which are listed at random (all the answers contain five letters). Fit the answers into the grid, going either across or down. There is a starter letter to help you on your way.

Clues

American composer Copland
An art form such as ballet
Describes music that is recorded and not 'live'
Tenor Sir Peter
Composer of the anthem 'I Was Glad'
A manner of performing

182 BACK TRACK

There are two clues to help you find two solutions. The first clue leads you to a general word. The second clue leads you to a music-based word. The solutions are very similar, but in the second word the middle letter has moved *backwards* in the alphabet.

RESTRICTING, TIGHT-FITTING UNDERGARMENTS

BRASS INSTRUMENTS

183 **INVISIBLES**

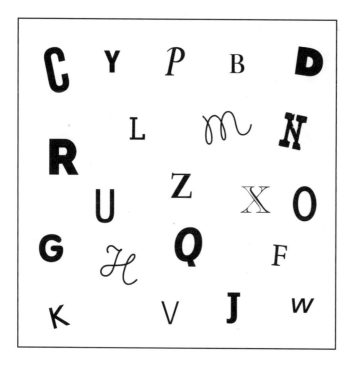

To solve this puzzle you need to use what you cannot see. Some letters of the alphabet do NOT appear in the box. Use each missing letter once to form the name of a composer.

184 **MOVIE A TO Z**

Here is the name of a movie with music that has featured in the Classic FM Hall of Fame – but the letters are shown in alphabetical order. Rearrange the letters to find a two-word movie title.

A A A C D E I I M N O P R S

185 **COMPOSING**

Put the seven-letter words below in the grid in the right order
to reveal the name of a famous composer in the diagonal
shaded squares.

1						
2						
3						
4						
5						
6						
7						

BRITTEN
FIDDLER
MARIMBA
RONDEAU
TUNEFUL
VESPERS
WHISTLE

186 **WHAT AM I?**

My first is in GAPS
But isn't in PAGE.
My second's in CASTS
But isn't in STAGE.
My third is in SOLO
And isn't in LEADS.
My fourth is in CHORUS
And is also in READS.
My fifth is in LESS
And is also in MORE.
I'm a musical book,
Need I say any more?

187 **SOUND BITE**

Solve the quick-fire clues below. The answers *sound* the same as five famous composers.

Clues
1   Feathered friend
2   Part of a door or drawer
3   GB national
4   Spine
5   Dreadful

188 **MUSIC BOX**

T	P	O	D	S	Z
P	O	Y	L	A	N
X	K	M	R	E	E
O	R	Q	R	M	K
R	A	S	A	E	L
J	B	S	O	L	V

In a word square, the same words can be read either across or down. Your challenge is to make a word square in the empty grid. Three of the four words you need are hiding in the letter box, each one in a straight line that can go in any direction. The fourth word is the name of a musical instrument – you must decide which one!

189 **BACH-WORDS**

The name of a composer is hidden in the sentence below, but it has been written backwards. Look for a continuous line of letters from right to left to spell out the name.

THE DANCER EXECUTED THE MOST EXQUISITE WALTZ, SILENTLY GLIDING ACROSS THE FLOOR.

190 QUIZ CROSSWORD

Work out the answer to each question in order to fill the grid.

Across

7   What is the surname of violinist Tasmin? (6)

9   *Arianna*, *Norma* and *Salome* are all types of which musical work? (6)

10   Which musical instruction means becoming quieter? (10)

11   Which word completes the name of the drama series, _ _ _ _ *of Thrones*, which includes the song 'Heroes'? (4)

12   What is the opening aria from Handel's *Xerxes*? (5)

13   Which instrument did Saint-Saëns use to represent rattling bones in *The Carnival of the Animals*? (9)

15   Which south American dances are chiefly associated with Argentina? (7)

20   Which word for a music ensemble, associated with Daniel Barenboim, completes the name, the West-Eastern Divan _ _ _ _ _ _ _ _ _? (9)

21   The koto and shamisen are musical instruments from which country? (5)

23   Which movie has music composed by Patrick Doyle, and includes the song 'Sons of Odin'? (4)

24   What name is given to pieces of music that are not live but can be listened to? (10)

25   Owning a collection of musical instruments through the ages, the V&A is a type of what? (6)

26   What is the English translation of *Cesare* in Handel's *Giulio Cesare in Egitto*? (6)

Down

1   What word describes the technology that allows opera houses to make performances available remotely? (7)

2   To which section of the orchestra do the viola and cello belong? (7)

3   Which of Holst's *Planets* was the bringer of peace? (5)

4   Which one-act ballet was choreographed by Sir Frederick Ashton, to music by Erik Satie? (9)

5   What do crotchets, quavers, and breves indicate – lengths or volumes of notes? (7)

6   What is the combining of notes at the same time to produce chords called? (7)

8   Who wrote *Symphony of Sorrowful Songs*? (6,7)

14   Which large orchestral instruments are usually struck with a stick? (4,5)

16   Who was in the Underworld in the Offenbach opera? (7)

17   What was the first name of American composer Ives? (7)

18   What is an afternoon performance of an opera or ballet called? (7)

19   What does the V stand for in the initials R.V.W.? (7)

22   What is one song or piece on a CD or LP called? (5)

191 **SPIRAL**

1			2		
		7			3
6					
	9			8	
5					4

Solve the clues and write your answers in a clockwise direction in the spiral grid. Each answer begins in a numbered space. The words overlap each other in the spiral, with at least the last letter of one answer becoming the first letter of the next.

Clues

1   Australian soprano Dame Nellie
2   A ukulele
3   First name of composer Haydn
4   Middle name of American associated with marches, John _____ Sousa
5   The Labeque sisters perform on this
6   US soprano Jessye
7   String instrument similar to a lute
8   This Jenny was known as the Swedish Nightingale
9   Spanish tenor Placido

192 **CIRCLES**

There are three circles and three words to be formed. The question mark stands for a mystery letter, which appears in all three words. Use all the letters in each circle once, including the mystery letter, to find the words.

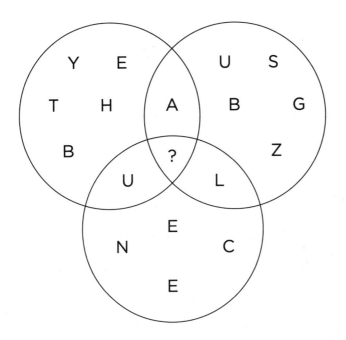

Clue
You are looking for three music festivals.

193 **THE LOST CHORD**

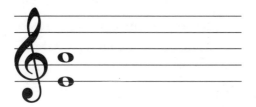

In a stave in the treble clef, the notes reading upwards in the spaces are F, A, C and E. The notes reading upwards on the lines are E, G, B, D and F. The sequence continues with notes above and below the stave.

Our stave shows a chord that has lost one note. The clue below leads to an answer made up of the letters of the notes shown in the stave, with an extra letter, A to G.

Can you find the missing note to complete the lost chord?

Clue
Something old brought about by Holst?

194 **ALPHA MALE**

The letters below make up the name of a male singer, but they are presented in alphabetical order. Rearrange the letters to reveal the singer's identity.

B E E F L N R R T Y

195 **SESTET**

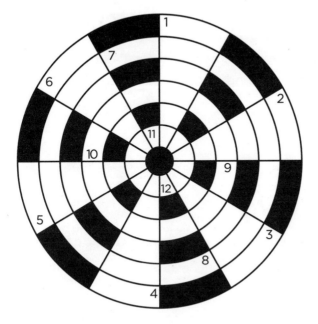

All answers have six letters. 1 to 6 start in the outer circle and are written towards the centre. 7 to 12 go around the rings in a clockwise direction.

Clues

1   The thieving bird in Rossini's opera
2   Word that completes the title of Tchaikovsky's work, _ _ _ _ _ _ *Onegin*?
3   The highest male voices
4   Composer Barber's first name
5   Name is given to a whole professional life
6   Place in Spain, home to the Teatro Real
7   Famous river that Strauss wrote about
8   Percussion instrument, usually played in pairs – a hollow container filled with beans and shaken
9   Control that makes something louder or quieter
10   Time with three beats to the bar
11   Another name for rhythmic patterns in music
12   Austrian pianist Brendel's first name

196 **TYPO**

Someone has made a mistake when preparing the programme for a concert. It's only one wrong letter, but it creates a new word and gives the title of the piece a whole new meaning! From the clue, can you identify the well-known work as it appears in the programme?

Clue
A one-word titled opera about a spicy dish of food.

197 **VOWEL PLAY**

The name of a music venue is shown without its vowels. Can you identify it?

L N D N C L S M

(Two words)

198 **ALPHA MALE**

The letters below make up the name of a male singer, but they are presented in alphabetical order. Rearrange the letters to reveal the singer's identity.

A D E E J L N O S

199 SUDO-KEY

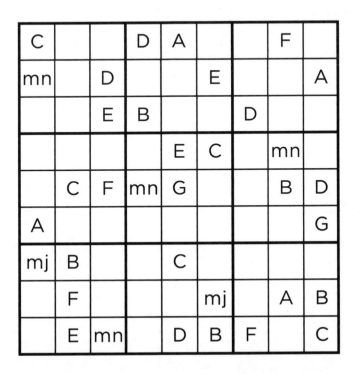

In this puzzle, each block of nine squares must contain the letters of the keys A, B, C, D, E, F and G, along with mj to denote a major key and mn to denote a minor key. Every row (going across) and every column (going down) must contain nine different keys.

200 NUMBER SUM

Test your musical knowledge and your basic arithmetic skills in one puzzle.

What number do you get if you multiply the number of Satie's *Gymnopédies* by the number of widows in the opera by Smetana?

201 **PERFECT FIFTH**

Solve the clues, which are listed at random. Each answer contains five letters. Complete the grid so that each answer starts in a space with an odd number and ends in the space with the even number that is one greater. To give you a perfect start, the letter in space 1 is E.

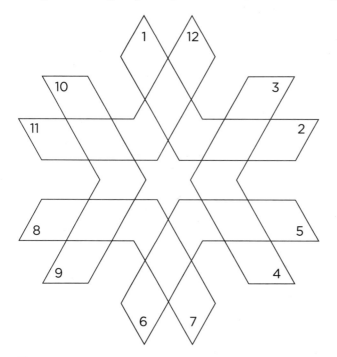

Clues
Fishers but not for fish
Another fish, but with strings attached
Catch the last post with this
Mezzo soprano, good with cakes
Conceal rude butler at first performance
Senior conductor

202 A QUIZ FOR CLASSICAL MUSIC EXPERTS

A fiendish musical quiz. If you get full marks, we'll be seriously impressed!

1 What is the name given to the lower register of the clarinet's playing range?
a)   Chalumeau
b)   Thalumeau
c)   Shalumeau
d)   Shalamar

2 What did Benjamin Britten use to simulate raindrops in his opera for amateur musicians, *Noye's Fludd*?
a)   Pipettes and buckets
b)   Empty baked beans tins
c)   Teacups on a string
d)   A typewriter

3 Who wrote the 'Skittle Alley Trio'?
a)   Wolfgang Amadeus Mozart
b)   George Gershwin
c)   Leonard Bernstein
d)   Antonín Dvořák

4 In French opera houses, what job does the Souffler have?
a)   To encourage applause
b)   Prompter
c)   First aider
d)   Dessert chef

5 What is Simon Rattle's middle name?
a)   Denis
b)   David
c)   Derek
d)   Daniel

203 MISSING VOICES

The voices are soprano, alto, tenor and bass. The letters S, A, T and B (or some of these letters) are missing in the words below. Can you identify the 'missing voice' letters to find the name of the work?

? H E   ? E ? ? O N ?

204 **NINTH SYMPHONY**

Each number from 1 to 9 represents a different letter of the alphabet. Solve the clues and write the letters in the correct spaces in the grid to reveal a music-related word or name.

1	2	3	4	5	6	7	8	9

Clues

a) Polish composer   956487

b) Film score by John Williams (*The*)   3811867

c) Handel's, *Did You Not See _ _ Lady?*   32

205 **FORTUNE TELLER**

The fortune teller can see into the future. Whose fortune is she telling here?

'You will study at the Royal College of Music and go on to write music for Post Office documentaries.

'You will write an opera to commemorate the Festival of Britain in 1951.

'You will establish a music festival on the Suffolk coast.'

206 **METRONOME**

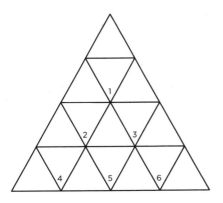

Each answer contains four letters. The first letter goes in a numbered triangle, the second letter directly above it, the third letter to the right and the fourth to the left.

Clues
1   First line of a carol, '_ _ _ _ in a manger'
2   Norwegian wanderer Peer _ _ _ _
3   Soprano Ms Upshaw's favourite time of day?
4   The lead in a show
5   Russian soprano, _ _ _ _ Netrebko
6   Pianists Christina and Michelle Naughton are _ _ _ _ sisters

207 **ADDERS**

Find two answers that can be added together to form a new word with a musical link.

What do you get if you add spoil to an organisation concerned with work-related matters?

208 HALF TIME

The clues below are listed at random, but they each have a four-letter answer. Solve the clues, then write the words into the grid so that the last two letters of one answer become the first two letters of the next. Each first letter appears in a numbered space.

1		2		3		4		5			

Clues

Adelaide Anne Procter's chord
Sound of ringing church bells
Work by Strauss, _ _ _ *Sprach Zarathustra*
Specific movement in a dance
Time when a singer or musician takes the limelight

209 DIMINUENDO

Here are three clues to the identity of a famous composer. The number of points you earn diminishes the more clues you use. You earn THREE points if you only use Clue 1, TWO points if you need Clue 2, and just ONE point if you need Clue 3 as well.

Clue 1: This composer was born on St Cecilia's day – which was appropriate, as she is the patron saint of music.

Clue 2: His *War Requiem* was commissioned for the consecration of the new Coventry Cathedral in 1962.

Clue 3: He was the first musician to receive a life peerage, and has a school named after him near Lowestoft in Suffolk.

210 **REARRANGEMENT**

There are two clues to help you find two solutions. The first clue leads you to a general word. The second clue leads you to a music-based word. You will need all your skills as an arranger, as the second word is an anagram of the first – it has all the same letters, but in a different order.

VERY KEEN, EAGER

PRIMA DONNA

211 **SPLIT PERSONALITY**

The letters in a composer's name have been split and rearranged. The composer's first name and surname both have six letters. The letters in each name remain in the correct order. Who is the composer?

T H T A L O M L A S I S

212 **OCTET**

Solve the clues below to find the eight-letter answers. The first letter of the answer goes in the numbered square, and the answer can go clockwise or anticlockwise. You must work out which direction it goes.

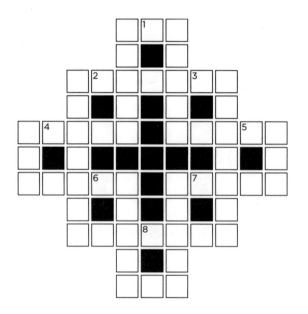

Clues

1   George or brother Ira
2   Tchaikovsky ballet that features Prince Siegfried and Odette (4,4)
3   Terracotta flutes that resemble elongated eggs
4   Formerly Miss Te Kanawa, but now with a title! (4,4)
5   The notes of a chord played separately, not simultaneously
6   Puccini opera first staged in Turin in 1896 – not well received (2,6)
7   Male voice, whose name comes from the Greek meaning 'deep sounding'
8   A musician with exceptional technical skill and talent

213 **CYMBALISM**

Individual letters have been replaced by symbols. The first row names an instrument, the second a composer, the third another instrument and the fourth another composer.

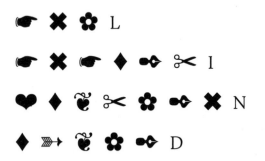

214 **IN HARMONY**

A university is running a summer course for intense studying and singing in four-part harmony.

There is a good response from applicants, who are eager to enrol. As usual, the ladies outnumber the gentlemen, but there is quite a healthy mix of voices.

A third of singers are sopranos and a quarter are altos. A fifth of singers are tenors and 26 bass voices are taking part.

How many singers are there altogether?

215 **INVISIBLES**

To solve this puzzle you need to use what you cannot see. Some letters of the alphabet do NOT appear in the box. Use each missing letter once to form the name of a composer.

216 HIDDEN INSTRUMENT

Which musical instrument is hidden in the sentence below? Discover it by joining words or parts of words together.

ALBERT PARTICULARLY ENJOYED THE STRINGS PLAYING ON GARDINER'S RECORDING OF THE MOZART OPERAS.

217 VOWEL PLAY

The name of a ballet is shown without its vowels. Can you identify it?

D N Q X T

(Two words)

218 PHONOGRAPH

Rearrange the letters to find the title of a long-established favourite from the concert repertoire. There are three words in the title.

WORTHY WIDER ME

219 NATURE NOTES WORD SEARCH

B	I	N	V	E	S	L	A	M	I	N	A
J	U	D	R	I	B	E	R	I	F	W	Q
Y	B	M	E	H	C	U	C	K	O	O	L
X	L	E	B	A	T	G	C	L	X	L	A
A	S	F	V	L	A	R	L	N	V	V	R
B	W	E	D	R	E	I	O	S	T	E	K
S	A	A	D	A	W	B	N	U	B	S	E
P	N	E	T	N	G	O	E	U	T	P	I
R	N	I	E	E	S	U	N	E	T	S	P
I	O	E	H	A	R	A	J	H	N	A	G
N	R	A	E	D	D	F	O	U	R	W	A
G	C	S	G	N	I	A	T	N	U	O	M

Find the names of words linked to nature from musical titles hidden in the word square. All the words are in straight lines that run horizontally, vertically or diagonally. They may read forwards or backwards. You are looking for the word in capitals.

Carnival of the ANIMALS
The Flight of the BUMBLEBEE
Fingal's CAVE
The CREATION
On Hearing the First CUCKOO in Spring
By the Beautiful Blue DANUBE
The FIREBIRD
The GADFLY
The Glorious GARDEN
The Banks of GREEN WILLOW

The LARK Ascending
The Thieving MAGPIE
Night on the Bare MOUNTAIN
The Four SEASONS
The Rite of SPRING
SWAN Lake
The TROUT
The WASPS
WATER Music
Dances With WOLVES

220 **FIVE FIT**

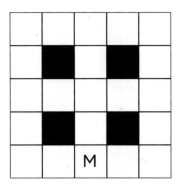

Solve the musical clues below, which are listed at random (all the answers contain five letters). Fit the answers into the grid, going either across or down. There is a starter letter to help you on your way.

Clues

A collection of pieces, a CD or an LP

The audience will do this when the 'Hallelujah' chorus is sung in *Messiah*

Lively European dance

Performs on a musical instrument

Star sign of Gershwin and Shostakovich

The Man in Jenkins' *A Mass for Peace*

221 **ENIGMA VARIATIONS**

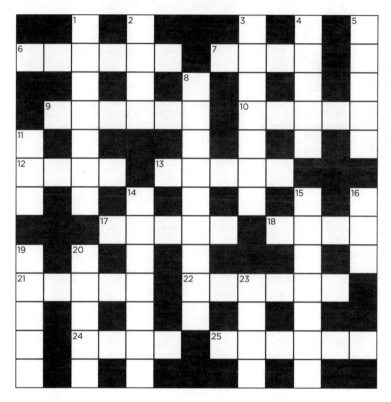

A cryptic crossword.

Across

6 Refrain in church or useful building (6)
7 Water for a swan (4)
9 Scour a fresh tenor (6)
10 No laity in this musical country (5)
12 Real change for King in Reimann's opera (4)
13 Delius's work written in rural fen by him, apparently (5)
17 Over indulgence by *Watermill* creator (5)
18 Arts create this leading light (4)
21 OK pal, we'll have a dance (5)
22 Tristan's partner is badly soiled (6)
24 Sounds like a Bletchley Park expert in the end passage (4)
25 Badly scratched, we hear, from the producer of *La Mer* (6)

Down

1 She sees her son at a series of concerts, playing these pieces (7)
2 Opera, not sung by this Scottish pop singer (4)
3 Rib Mama about playing these bars (7)
4 Plead earnestly to put the foot on this (5)
5 Dolly rearranges the middle name of the cellist (5)
8 Oh, ring Len to go to Wagnerian opera (9)
11 Gad about and this remains by Shostakovich (3)
14 Ian due I understand – Italian at the keyboard (7)
15 Ida must construct the large musical venue (7)
16 Sea-going vessel that survived *Noye's Fludde* (3)
19 Change paces between the lines (5)
20 Time for Haydn Symphony (5)
23 Not a solo performance by capital Norwegian such as Grieg (4)

222 **FILLERS**

Here are three words with the same letters missing. Find a single music-linked word to complete the longer words.

M _ _ _ _ _ A T I C

D I S _ _ _ _ _ I S E D

_ _ _ _ _ I C

223 **NUMBER NAMES**

Each letter has been given a numerical value from 1 to 6. The total value of each word is reached by adding up the individual letters. No two letters have the same number.

C A N - C A N = 12

C A S T = 13

C A N T A T A = 16

A C C E N T = 19

What is the value of

C A S T A N E T S ?

224 **RING CYCLE**

Solve the clues below, which are in no particular order, and slot the seven-letter answers into their correct places in the ring. The last letter of one answer forms the first letter of the next. Answer 1 begins with the letter S.

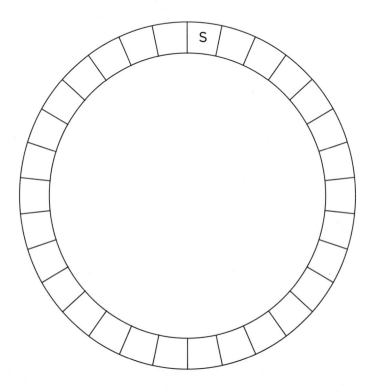

Clues
English composer of *The Whale* and *Thérèse*
Discs
A passage selected from a larger work
Chief of Police in Puccini's *Tosca*
Rework or adapt a composition

225 **CIRCLES**

There are three circles and three words to be formed. The question mark stands for a mystery letter, which appears in all three words. Use all the letters in each circle once, including the mystery letter, to find the words.

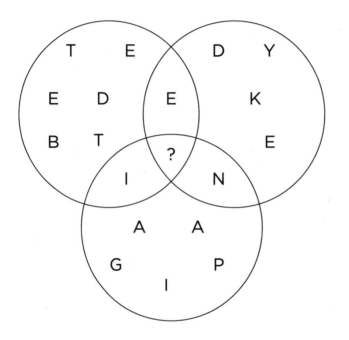

Clue
You are looking for the surnames of three violinists

226 **HEXACHORD**

All answers have six letters. They can be written in the grid either clockwise or anticlockwise around the clue number. The first letter of Clue 1 is in place.

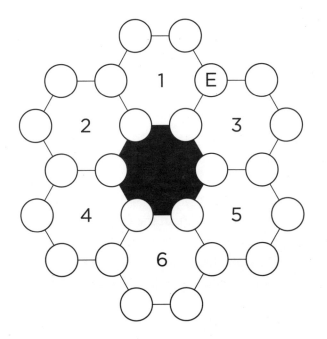

Clues

1. The name of Beethoven's third symphony
2. The instrument Nicola Benedetti plays
3. The word that completes the title of Mendelssohn's song: 'Hear My _ _ _ _ _ _'
4. The city in which opera composer Michael Balfe was born
5. Another name for an instrumentalist
6. A word that can be used for records such as LPs

227 **MUSIC BOX**

G	P	U	H	S	N
B	O	Y	L	L	N
L	L	M	R	E	E
O	R	U	Q	W	K
Z	A	S	E	H	L
E	B	B	S	L	J

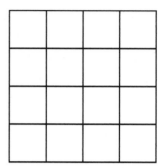

In a word square, the same words can be read either across or down. Your challenge is to make a word square in the empty grid. Three of the four words you need are hiding in the letter box, each one in a straight line that can go in any direction. The fourth word is the name of a musical instrument – you must decide which one!

228 **MOVIE A TO Z**

Here is the name of a movie with music that has featured in the Classic FM Hall of Fame – but the letters are shown in alphabetical order. Rearrange the letters to find a two-word movie title.

A C D G H I O O O R T V Z

229 NAME CHECK

Look at the clues below, which are in no particular order. Write the answer to each clue horizontally in the grid. You need to work out the correct order so that the shaded columns reveal the first name and surname of an English composer.

1					
2					
3					
4					
5					
6					
7					

Clues

Watered down
Fled from captivity
French castle, especially along the Loire
Restricted, confined
Sad, miserable
Ghost
First letter of a name

230 **PRESTO**

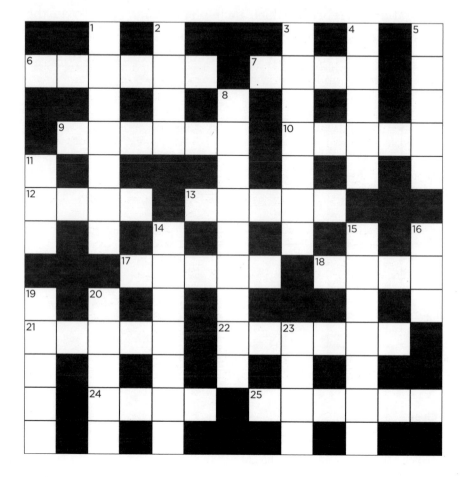

A classic quick crossword.

Across

6 Bradford-born composer of *On Hearing the First Cuckoo in Spring* (6)

7 A leading light in music performance (4)

9 Legendary violinist Menuhin (6)

10 A player may do this if he/she departs from the set music (2,3)

12 Name shared by organist Jackson and composer Orff (4)

13 Writer of rousing American marches (5)

17 British mezzo soprano Dame Janet (5)

18 Puccini aria 'One _ _ _ _ Day' (4)

21 European dance (5)

22 Musical fork to make sure the notes are at a correct pitch (6)

24 Rossini's hero William (4)

25 Sequences of notes in ascending or descending order (6)

Down

1 Instruction to play in a lively tempo (7)

2 Ballerina's dress (4)

3 Austrian family of dance musicians who popularised the waltz (7)

4 A rapid alternation of notes, also called a shake (5)

5 Dame Nellie, born Helen Porter Mitchell (5)

8 Opera by Verdi, which has a court jester as the name in the title (9)

11 A division of an operetta or opera (3)

14 Born in the city, she sang 'Barcelona' with Freddie Mercury at the Barcelona Olympics (7)

15 An early automatic keyboard instrument (7)

16 It may be major or minor (3)

19 Birth country of Placido Domingo (5)

20 Woodwind instrument (5)

23 Part of the violin that bears the finger board (4)

231 **NUMBER SUM**

Test your musical knowledge and your basic arithmetic skills in one puzzle.

What number do you get if you add Shostakovich's *Unforgettable Year* to the number who share the singing of Bizet's *Pearl Fishers*?

232 **FAST FORWARD**

There are two clues to help you find two solutions. The first clue leads you to a general word. The second clue leads you to a music-based word. The solutions are very similar, but in the second word the middle letter has moved *forwards* in the alphabet.

FRIGHTEN

THE MUSIC COMPOSED FOR A FILM OR PLAY

233 **WHAT AM I?**

My first is in LEARNS
But is not in RECALLS.
My second's in SOARS
But is not found in FALLS.
My third is in PITCH
But is not found in PLACE.
My fourth is in TIME
And is also in SPACE.

234 SPIRAL

1				2	
					3
6					
	9			7	
5		8			
				4	

Solve the clues and write your answers in a clockwise direction in the spiral grid. Each answer begins in a numbered space. The words overlap each other in the spiral, with at least the last letter of one answer becoming the first letter of the next.

Clues

1   Iannis, who wrote *Metastasis*
2   Musical adapted from classical pieces by Borodin
3   Czech composer, the first major nationalist composer of Bohemia
4   A note that is neither sharp not flat
5   Low female voice
6   Conductor who gave the first performance of *La bohème*
7   Violinist Kennedy
8   Composer of the *Pomp and Circumstance* marches
9   Delius took a 'Walk to the Paradise' what?

235 **I WAS THERE**

Look at the world event below and the names of the three composers. Using your knowledge of when the composers lived, which of them could have said, 'I was there'?

YURI GAGARIN BECAME THE FIRST MAN IN SPACE

Bela Bartók
Arnold Schoenberg
Dmitri Shostakovich

236 **MISS HERD**

There is nothing Miss Herd likes more than listening in to other people's conversations. Unfortunately, she sometimes confuses words that sound the same but have different meanings. Can you help her out and correct the statement below? There are THREE words to change.

AT THE AFTER-SHOW REFRESHMENTS IN THE CHURCH HALL, THERE WAS MUCH PRAISE FOR THE POPULAR *NUTCRACKER* SWEET. THE NEWLY DIVORCED SOPRANO, WHO LIKED RELIGIOUS MUSIC, WAS IN A LENGTHY DISCUSSION ABOUT A CHANGE OF HIM. IN A CHURCH, ALL AGREED THAT THE PEEL OF THE BELLS GIVES AN ADDED DIMENSION TO THE MUSIC.

237 **PERFECT FIFTH**

Solve the clues, which are listed at random. Each answer contains five letters. Complete the grid so that each answer starts in a space with an odd number and ends in the space with the even number that is one greater. To give you a perfect start, the letter in space 1 is S.

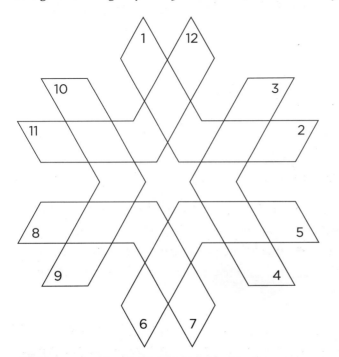

Clues
Bulb illuminating music that is easy to listen to
Chant but very ordinary
Seem to call it a lyric from Pavarotti's homeland
Dance on the Danube
Film score composer on the beach
Reverie on a night at the end of June

238 **SESTET**

All answers have six letters. 1 to 6 start in the outer circle and are written towards the centre. 7 to 12 go around the rings in a clockwise direction.

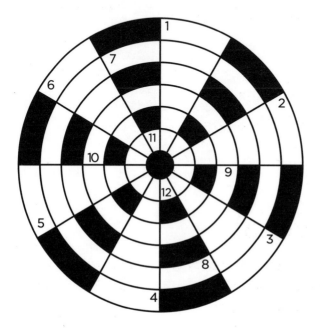

Clues

1   Welsh bass baritone Bryn who was the second recipient of the Queen's Medal for Music
2   What follows record, cassette and CD in terms of music machines
3   William Walton was born in Oldham but he dies on this island
4   Gifts that are a part of Aaron Copland's *Appalachian Spring*
5   A shade of meaning, a subtlety
6   Tenor compatriot of Clue 1, with surname Burrows
7   Instruments associated with Jacqueline du Pré and Sheku Kanneh-Mason?
8   French dance famous at the court of Louis XIV
9   Polish composer, with a French father, most famous for his work for piano
10 Suite by Shostakovich from his *Romance*
11 Beginning of the hymn of praise that ends 'in excelsis Deo'?
12 In music notation, this is signified by double bars with vertical pairs of dots

239 **NINTH SYMPHONY**

Each number from 1 to 9 represents a different letter of the alphabet. Solve the clues and write the letters in the correct spaces in the grid to reveal a music-related word or name.

1	2	3	4	5	6	7	8	9

Clues

a) Czech composer, who married Dvořák's daughter   658
b) Large, plucked string instrument   7941
c) English composer Maxwell Davies   12324

240 **BACH-WORDS**

The name of a composer is hidden in the sentence below, but it has been written backwards. Look for a continuous line of letters from right to left to spell out the name.

ALBERT PLAYED THE FIDDLE, VARYING THE PIECES BETWEEN THE TRADITIONAL AND MODERN REPERTOIRE.

241 **MUSICAL TASTES**

Sally and William prefer operetta to opera. Their favourite instrument in the woodwind section is the piccolo and they also like the bassoon. Of the four main voices, which do you think they will like the best and why?

242 **BACK TRACK**

There are two clues to help you find two solutions. The first clue leads you to a general word. The second clue leads you to a music-based word. The solutions are very similar, but in the second word the middle letter has moved *backwards* in the alphabet.

SPORTING FIXTURE

PIECE OF MILITARY MUSIC

243 **HALF TIME**

The clues below are listed at random, but they each have a four-letter answer. Solve the clues, then write the words into the grid so that the last two letters of one answer become the first two letters of the next. Each first letter appears in a numbered space.

1		2		3		4		5			

Clues
Prepare a manuscript ready for printing
Alternative word for *Bald* in the title *Night on Bald Mountain*
Substantial instrument in the brass section
Part of a clarinet
Individual piece of music featured as part of a concert

244 SUDO-KEY

		mj	E		mn			C
		E		mj		D		
		B	G		C	mn		
		G	C		F	E		
	D						G	
E								A
		mn	F		mj	G	A	
	A			mn			mj	
G								B

In this puzzle, each block of nine squares must contain the letters of the keys A, B, C, D, E, F and G, along with mj to denote a major key and mn to denote a minor key. Every row (going across) and every column (going down) must contain nine different keys.

245 **NOTATION**

Each letter that appears in the treble clef (A, B, C, D, E, F and G) has been replaced by a musical note. The other letters of the alphabet are in place. Can you work out the name of the composer and a piece of their music?

P ♪ ♪ H ♪ L ♪ ♪ L

♪ ♪ N O N   ♪ N ♪   ♪ I ♪ U ♪

246 **FORTUNE TELLER**

The fortune teller can see into the future. Whose fortune is she telling here?

'You will win an Austrian national prize for your Symphony No. 3 and Brahms will be on the jury.

'In 1892, you will be lured to the USA, to the National Conservatory of Music, with a salary of $15,000 – twenty times what you were paid in your homeland!

'Your Ninth Symphony will have its première at Carnegie Hall in 1893 to great acclaim.'

247 **THE LOST CHORD**

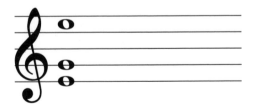

In a stave in the treble clef, the notes reading upwards in the spaces are F, A, C and E. The notes reading upwards on the lines are E, G, B, D and F. The sequence continues with notes above and below the stave.

Our stave shows a chord that has lost one note. The clue below leads to an answer made up of the letters of the notes shown in the stave, with an extra letter, A to G.

Can you find the missing note to complete the lost chord?

Clue
Move cautiously with part of Vaughan Williams' song cycle?

248 **SPLIT PERSONALITY**

The letters in a composer's name have been split and rearranged. The composer's first name and surname both have six letters. The letters in each name remain in the correct order. Who is the composer?

P I B E O R U R E L E Z

249 **INVISIBLES**

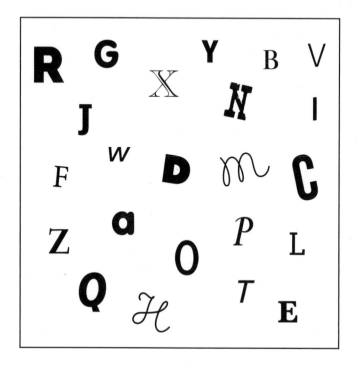

To solve this puzzle you need to use what you cannot see. Some letters of the alphabet do NOT appear in the box. Use each missing letter once to form the name of a composer.

250 **ALPHA MALE**

The letters below make up the name of a male singer, but they are presented in alphabetical order. Rearrange the letters to reveal the singer's identity.

A D D D E E E F I M M O O R S T

251 **REARRANGEMENT**

There are two clues to help you find two solutions. The first clue leads you to a general word. The second clue leads you to a music-based word. You will need all your skills as an arranger, as the second word is an anagram of the first – it has all the same letters, but in a different order.

HAVING MORE FLAVOUR

A PROFESSIONAL SINGER OR DANCER

252 **TYPO**

Someone has made a mistake when preparing the programme for a concert. It's only one wrong letter, but it creates a new word and gives the title of the piece a whole new meaning! From the clue, can you identify the well-known work as it appears in the programme?

Clue
Major work about a mythological flying two-wheeler.

253 **CIRCLES**

There are three circles and three words to be formed. The question mark stands for a mystery letter, which appears in all three words. Use all the letters in each circle once, including the mystery letter, to find the words.

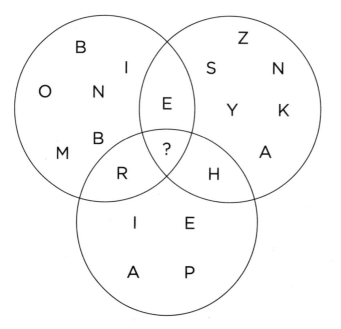

Clue
You are looking for the surnames of three pianists.

254 **ADDERS**

Find two answers that can be added together to form a new word with a musical link.

What do you get if you add a saint to items of jewellery?

255 **COMPOSING**

Put the seven-letter words below in the grid into the right order to reveal the name of a famous composer in the diagonal shaded squares.

1						
2						
3						
4						
5						
6						
7						

BALLADS
GORECKI
MARACAS
PICCOLO
POPULAR
REVISED
VIOLINS

256 **METRONOME**

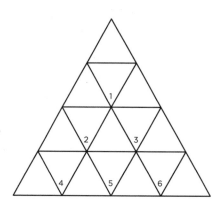

Each answer contains four letters. The first letter goes in a numbered triangle, the second letter directly above it, the third letter to the right and the fourth to the left.

Clues

1 English conductor Sir Henry, famed for his sea shanties
2 Lyrical poems often set to music
3 The soul of genius, according to Mozart
4 Capital city where Grieg lived
5 Hollow cup-shaped instrument
6 In *Sleeping Beauty* Maleficent is the 'Mistress of all _ _ _ _'

257 **HIDDEN INSTRUMENT**

Which musical instrument is hidden in the sentence below? Discover it by joining words or parts of words together.

THE OPEN AIR CONCERT WILL BE CALLED OFF IF EVERY PERFORMER IS WORRIED ABOUT THE IMPENDING THUNDERSTORM.

258 **DIMINUENDO**

Here are three clues to the identity of a famous composer. The number of points you earn diminishes the more clues you use. You earn THREE points if you only use Clue 1, TWO points if you need Clue 2, and just ONE point if you need Clue 3 as well.

Clue 1: This composer was born in Los Angeles in 1912, and worked as a dance accompanist.

Clue 2: He sometimes used to fry mushrooms on stage.

Clue 3: He performed a piece for 4 minutes, 33 seconds, where no additional sound was produced other than what was in the auditorium.

259 **WHAT AM I?**

My first is in ECHO
And also in CALL.
My second's in HALF
But isn't in ALL.
My third is in CAROL
And is also in SONG.
My fourth is RIGHT
And is also in WRONG.
My fifth is in VIDEO
But isn't in VOTES.
I always am formed
With the joining of notes.

260 **NAME CHECK**

Look at the clues below, which are in no particular order. Write the answer to each clue horizontally in the grid. You need to work out the correct order so that the shaded columns reveal the first name and surname of an Austrian composer.

1				
2				
3				
4				

Clues
Greek island
Private teacher
Nimble, quick-moving
Item worn around the shoulders or for wrapping a baby

261 **FILLERS**

Here are three words with the same letters missing. Find a single music-linked word to complete the longer words.

Q U I C K T _ _ _ _

T _ _ _ _ B I L L

S _ _ _ _

262 **GAMERS**

At a gathering of gamers, there's a meeting for composers who create the musical soundtracks for the games.

Jeff Gold, Tom Grey and Sara Silver sit down and have a chat during a coffee break. Their name badges reveal they each have a surname that is a colour.

The composers' newest offerings are: *A Goblet Full of Gold, Escape from the Silver Sentinel* and *The Curse of the Grey-Haired Prophet.*

'How weird is it that we share surnames that are colours?' asks Jeff Gold.

'What's more of a coincidence is that these three colours appear in our game titles, but no one has their own surname in a title they have worked on,' replies the composer who had written *Escape From the Silver Sentinel.*

Match the composers to their works.

263 **PHONOGRAPH**

Rearrange the letters to find the title of a long-established favourite from the concert repertoire. There are four words in the title.

FRIED TOMATOES HUNGER

264 **OCTET**

Solve the clues below to find the eight-letter answers. The first letter of the answer goes in the numbered square, and the answer can go clockwise or anticlockwise. You must work out which direction it goes.

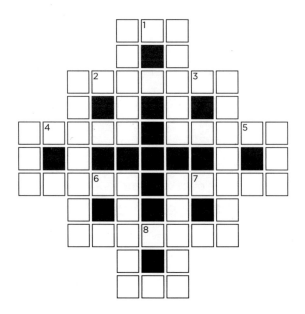

Clues

1 Section of the orchestra where you would find oboes and bassoons
2 Violinist who mutilated his hand to increase the spread of his fingers
3 US composer who wrote *Violanta* and Hollywood film scores
4 Vaughan Williams composed his _____ *Antarctica* after creating the music for the film *Scott of the Antarctic*
5 A plucked stringed instrument
6 His operetta collaborator was W S Gilbert
7 Name given to Beethoven's sixth symphony
8 You would find this instrument in the same section as Clue 1

265 **FIVE FIT**

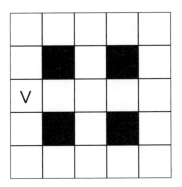

Solve the musical clues below, which are listed at random (all the answers contain five letters). Fit the answers into the grid, going either across or down. There is a starter letter to help you on your way.

Clues

Conductor Sir Georg, who was ten years at Covent Garden
Leading ladies – the temperamental sort?
Set of instrumental pieces such as *The Planets*
Records, played on a gramophone
Control on a brass instrument
Subdivision of an act in an opera

266 **RING CYCLE**

Solve the clues below, which are in no particular order, and slot
the seven-letter answers into their correct places in the ring.
The last letter of one answer forms the first letter of the next.
Answer 1 begins with the letter H.

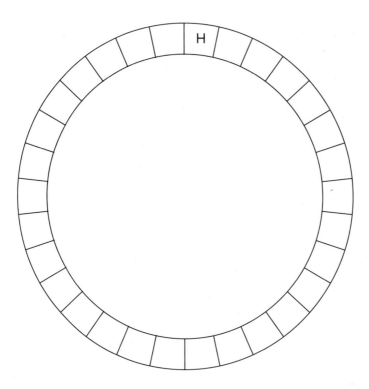

Clues

Clap in appreciation

Overture and suite for orchestra by Sibelius

Dutch conductor who became musical director at Covent Garden in 1987

The Bolshoi, the Kirov and Sadler's Wells have all had these types of performers

Haydn's *Le Midi* has this number in the very long list of Haydn symphonies

267 **CYMBALISM**

Individual letters have been replaced by symbols. The first row names an instrument, the second a composer, the third and fourth rows are both movements from *The Planets*.

268 **NUMBER NAMES**

Each letter has been given a numerical value from 1 to 6. The total value of each word is reached by adding up the individual letters. No two letters have the same number.

D I D O = 7

T R I O = 14

R A D I O = 17

T R I A D = 19

What is the value of

O R A T O R I O ?

269 **MUSIC BOX**

Z	P	U	H	J	O
U	P	O	N	L	P
L	S	M	R	E	U
O	R	E	Q	U	S
Z	A	G	N	E	X
V	U	B	S	D	T

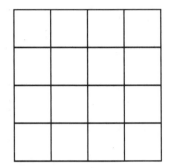

In a word square, the same words can be read either across or down. Your challenge is to make a word square in the empty grid. Three of the four words you need are hiding in the letter box, each one in a straight line that can go in any direction. The fourth word is the name of a musical instrument – you must decide which one!

270 **FAST FORWARD**

There are two clues to help you find two solutions. The first clue leads you to a general word. The second clue leads you to a music-based word. The solutions are very similar, but in the second word the middle letter has moved *forwards* in the alphabet.

EVERGREEN TREES

TUBES THAT PRODUCE SOUND IN AN ORGAN

271 SPIRAL

1					2
			6		
5				7	3
		8			
			4		

Solve the clues and write your answers in a clockwise direction in the spiral grid. Each answer begins in a numbered space. The words overlap each other in the spiral, with at least the last letter of one answer becoming the first letter of the next.

Clues

1   Argentine cellist Sol
2   Latin dance
3   Howard who wrote *Eternal Light: A Requiem*
4   In a lively tempo
5   He composed *Concierto de Aranjuez*
6   Italian baritone Tito
7   He is famous for *The Watermill*
8   George or Ira

272 **QUICK QUOTE**

	A	B	C	D	E	F	G
1							
2							
3							
4							
5							
6							
7							

Solve the quick clues and write your answers across in the grid.

Clues
1   Previn was best known as this kind of instrumentalist
2   One of the many kinds of entertainment he was associated with, such as *My Fair Lady*
3   Instrumental music, usually for three to eight players
4   Play in front of an audience
5   Making a movie
6   The Previn family moved to Los _____ in 1939
7   He was conductor-in-chief of this Texas symphony orchestra in 1967–70

Now, using the grid references (A1, B5, etc.), take the letter from the space indicated and write it below to reveal a quotation. This is a quote from André Previn, describing the work of a conductor in 'making sure everyone is playing at the same speed and the same volume'.

E3.B4.B1.F5.C6   G1.A7.F6   E7.C4.F2.D4.A5.D2.A3   E2.F7.A1

_____   _____   _____   _____

273 I WAS THERE

Look at the world event below and the names of the three composers. Using your knowledge of when the composers lived, which of them could have said, 'I was there'?

THE BROTHERS GRIMM PRODUCED THEIR FIRST VOLUME OF FAIRY TALES

Joseph Haydn
Wolfgang Amadeus Mozart
Franz Schubert

274 BACK TRACK

There are two clues to help you find two solutions. The first clue leads you to a general word. The second clue leads you to a music-based word. The solutions are very similar, but in the second word the middle letter has moved *backwards* in the alphabet.

TOWN IN SOUTH-WEST SCOTLAND

MELODY

275 MOVIE A TO Z

Here is the name of a movie with music that has featured in the Classic FM Hall of Fame – but the letters are shown in alphabetical order. Rearrange the letters to find a three-word movie title.

A A A E G I I N N P R R S T V V Y

276 QUIZ CROSSWORD

Work out the answer to each question in order to fill the grid.

Across

7 What was the surname of legendary tenor Enrico? (6)

9 What is the Dame of percussion's first name? (6)

10 If T = tone and S = semitone, what is TTSTTTS? (5,5)

11 What is the first name of composer Coates? (4)

12 Which word completes the name of the film, where Rachmaninov's music made such a profound addition to the soundtrack, _ _ _ _ _ *Encounter*? (5)

13 What name is given to the historical era between 1901 and 1910, when Elgar wrote the first of his *Pomp and Circumstance* pieces? (9)

15 What is a more familiar name for a violinist? (7)

20 Which comedian Eric famously 'played' Grieg's Piano Concerto with André Previn? (9)

21 What name is given to a specific location for a concert? (5)

23 How many performers play in a quartet? (4)

24 What is the general name for a musical device that produces sounds? (10)

25 What was Clara Schumann's husband called? (6)

26 What is the first name of conductor Barenboim? (6)

Down

1 Which kind of Danse is Saint-Saëns known for? (7)

2 Which word means taught or educated, often on an individual basis? (7)

3 Which surname is shared by Gustav and his daughter Imogen? (5)

4 Which songs are sung to loved ones, usually out of doors at twilight? (9)

5 How are great performers, with some longevity, often known? (7)

6 Which term is used to describe words that resemble poetry? (7)

8 Who wrote *La Mer* after fleeing to Eastbourne with his mistress? (6,7)

14 Who are in the last round of a competition? (9)

16 Which Handel oratorio is about a wise Old Testament character? (7)

17 Which Kathleen was a renowned contralto, whose final performance was at Covent Garden before her early death in 1953? (7)

18 In which country was Jonas Kaufmann born? (7)

19 What follows *Trout* in the title of the Schubert composition? (7)

22 Which word completes the film title with a soundtrack by Dario Marianelli, _ _ _ _ _ *& Prejudice*? (5)

277 **SESTET**

All answers have six letters. 1 to 6 start in the outer circle and are written towards the centre. 7 to 12 go around the rings in a clockwise direction.

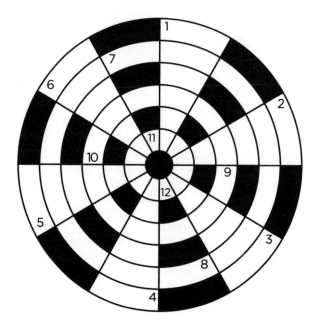

Clues

1 Art form of *The Nutcracker* and *Coppélia*
2 Elgar's first name
3 Caruso's first name
4 Frank, who wrote *The Sea* and was a teacher of Benjamin Britten
5 If a note goes up the scale, it is said to do this
6 American Cole who went to law school and also joined the French Foreign Legion
7 The subject of a Ketelby composition, *In a Monastery* _____
8 Musical term meaning quick or fast
9 Another name for a violin
10 Word that preceded '90' in the name of the football tournament at which the Three Tenors found fame
11 Where a music recording takes place
12 Principal violinist in an orchestra

278 **BACH-WORDS**

The name of a composer is hidden in the sentence below, but it has been written backwards. Look for a continuous line of letters from right to left to spell out the name.

WILLIAM STRODE ON TO THE STAGE, ALBEIT AS SOLO VIOLINIST RATHER THAN CONDUCTOR FOR THIS PERFORMANCE.

279 **ALPHA MALE**

The letters below make up the name of a male singer, but they are presented in alphabetical order. Rearrange the letters to reveal the singer's identity.

A A A C I I L N O O P R T T U V

280 **PHONOGRAPH**

Rearrange the letters to find the title of a long-established favourite from the concert repertoire. There are three words in the title.

A B E E H U T
B U N D L E

281 **THE LOST CHORD**

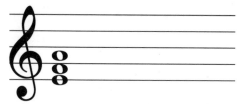

In a stave in the treble clef, the notes reading upwards in the spaces are F, A, C and E. The notes reading upwards on the lines are E, G, B, D and F. The sequence continues with notes above and below the stave.

Our stave shows a chord that has lost one note. The clue below leads to an answer made up of the letters of the notes shown in the stave, with an extra letter, A to G.

Can you find the missing note to complete the lost chord?

Clue
Meeting place for a society made up of writers, composers and painters.

282 **NINTH SYMPHONY**

Each number from 1 to 9 represents a different letter of the alphabet. Solve the clues and write the letters in the correct spaces in the grid to reveal a music-related word or name.

1	2	3	4	5	6	7	8	9

Clues
a) Recurring idea or melody   12343
b) Verdi opera   7587
c) Comic character in the mystery work   6969

283 SUDO-KEY

			E	G			
	mj		mn	A			C	
			B				D	
C		B			F			E
G								B
A					E	C		G
	B			F				
			G		C			
	C		E	D			mn	

In this puzzle, each block of nine squares must contain the letters of the keys A, B, C, D, E, F and G, along with mj to denote a major key and mn to denote a minor key. Every row (going across) and every column (going down) must contain nine different keys.

284 VOWEL PLAY

The name of a music venue is shown without its vowels. Can you identify it?

B L S H T H T R

(Two words)

285 **HEXACHORD**

All answers have six letters. They can be written in the grid either clockwise or anticlockwise around the clue number. The first letter of Clue 1 is in place.

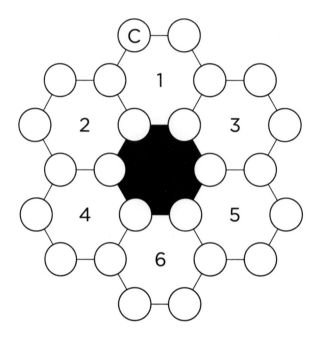

Clues

1   One-time scandalous dance written by Offenbach for *Orpheus in the Underworld* (3,3)
2   The third of Vivaldi's *Four Seasons*
3   Composer who had a notorious affair with novelist George Sand
4   Expression meaning having the correct pitch (2,4)
5   Composer who wrote the movie music for *Braveheart*
6   Word meaning to start staging productions again after a period of closure

286 **PERFECT FIFTH**

Solve the clues, which are listed at random. Each answer contains five letters. Complete the grid so that each answer starts in a space with an odd number and ends in the space with the even number that is one greater. To give you a perfect start, the letter in space 1 is B.

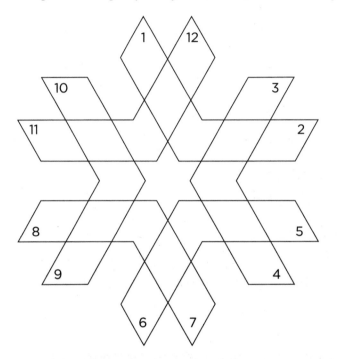

Clues

Remove coats at the opera
The result is a piece of printed music
The tale Harry revealed about a composer of operetta
Plunders, we hear, old instruments
Tutor confused about a Schubert favourite
French bread for conductor

287 **FORTUNE TELLER**

The fortune teller can see into the future. Whose fortune is she telling here?

'Brooklyn-born, you will head to Paris to be tutored for four years by Nadia Boulanger.

'Your famous *Fanfare* will be premiered in March 1943, "at income tax time", in order to raise revenue for the war effort.

'You will be investigated by the McCarthy Committee over suspected communist sympathies.'

288 **REARRANGEMENT**

There are two clues to help you find two solutions. The first clue leads you to a general word. The second clue leads you to a music-based word. You will need all your skills as an arranger, as the second word is an anagram of the first – it has all the same letters, but in a different order.

STORY IN A NEWSPAPER OR MAGAZINE

PERFORMANCE OF A PROGRAMME OF MUSIC

289 **CIRCLES**

There are three circles and three words to be formed. The question mark stands for a mystery letter, which appears in all three words. Use all the letters in each circle once, including the mystery letter, to find the words.

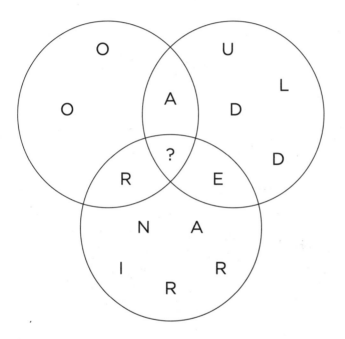

Clue
You are looking for the surnames of three conductors.

290 **MISSING VOICES**

The voices are soprano, alto, tenor and bass. The letters S, A, T and B (or some of these letters) are missing in the words below. Can you identify the 'missing voice' letters to find the name of the work?

? ? ? ? ? ?   M ? ? E R

291 **HALF TIME**

The clues below are listed at random, but they each have a four-letter answer. Solve the clues, then write the words into the grid so that the last two letters of one answer become the first two letters of the next. Each first letter appears in a numbered space.

1		2		3		4		5			

Clues

Clarinettist Ms Johnson
Literary work that can be set to music
Edwardian operetta, *The _ _ _ of the Mountains*
Device to raise the pitch of strings on a guitar
New and original thought

292 **NUMBER SUM**

Test your musical knowledge and your basic arithmetic skills in one puzzle.

What number do you get if you multiply the number of Dvořák's *Theme from the New World* by the number of lines on a stave?

293 **ADDERS**

Find two answers that can be added together to form a new word with a musical link.

What do you get if you add a salesman to a command to stand?

294 **SEATING PLAN**

S			A
	T		
B			T

The local operatic society is hosting a sight-reading workshop. There are 16 people attending and they happen to be four sopranos, four altos, four tenors and four bass singers. The organiser decides to make sure the voice ranges are evenly spread, and comes up with a seating plan of four rows of four seats. The aim is to have each row, column and diagonals from corner to corner containing one soprano, one alto, one tenor and one bass.

Five people are already in place. Can you complete the plan?

295 **NOTATION**

Each letter that appears in the treble clef (A, B, C, D, E, F and G) has been replaced by a musical note. The other letters of the alphabet are in place. Can you work out the name of the composer and a piece of their music?

♪ ♪ L I ♪ ♪ S

♪ O P P ♪ L I ♪

296 **NAME CHECK**

Look at the clues below, which are in no particular order. Write the answer to each clue horizontally into the grid. You need to work out the correct order so that the shaded columns reveal the first name and surname of an English composer born in the 16th century.

1						
2						
3						
4						
5						
6						
7						

Clues

Flowers on a fruit tree
Venetian boat
Idea, notion
News, information
Bush that produces blackberries
Describes something that dissolves in water
Pleasant, sociable

297 'JERUSALEM' WORD SEARCH

C	L	O	U	D	E	D	A	S	E	E	N
D	O	X	E	B	B	G	E	M	I	T	H
I	S	U	M	E	H	R	I	O	K	O	K
V	X	A	N	G	U	L	P	U	L	S	R
I	L	J	N	T	L	L	D	N	A	X	A
N	R	O	S	S	E	E	P	T	W	N	D
E	M	A	L	A	D	N	A	A	C	S	E
A	P	L	S	L	E	N	A	I	S	H	R
K	I	A	I	E	I	D	E	N	O	I	E
H	N	U	R	C	A	N	O	S	C	N	H
T	B	G	R	R	T	F	E	E	T	E	L
J	O	K	M	E	L	A	S	U	R	E	J

Find the names of words from the famous anthem 'Jerusalem' hidden in the word square. All the words are in straight lines that run horizontally, vertically or diagonally. They may read forwards or backwards. You are looking for the words in capitals.

And did those FEET in ANCIENT TIME
WALK upon England's MOUNTAINS GREEN?
And was the holy LAMB of God
On England's PLEASANT PASTURES SEEN?
And did the COUNTENANCE DIVINE
SHINE forth upon our CLOUDED HILLS?
And was JERUSALEM BUILDED HERE
AMONG these DARK SATANIC MILLS?

298 **METRONOME**

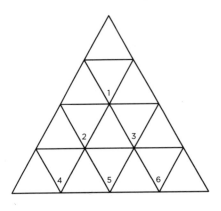

Each answer contains four letters. The first letter goes in a numbered triangle, the second letter directly above it, the third letter to the right and the fourth to the left.

Clues

1. Borodin's *In the Steppes of Central* _ _ _ _
2. Rock formation on the Isle of Staffa, which inspired Mendelssohn
3. A chicken dish and a musical *Great Gate*
4. Present-day saxophonist Ms Gillam
5. Insurance agent and American composer Charles
6. Lead cousin in *HMS Pinafore*

299 **SPLIT PERSONALITY**

The letters in a composer's name have been split and rearranged. The composer's first name and surname both have six letters. The letters in each name remain in the correct order. Who is the composer?

G M A U S H L T A V E R

300 **INVISIBLES**

To solve this puzzle you need to use what you cannot see. Some letters of the alphabet do NOT appear in the box. Use each missing letter once to form the name of a composer.

301 **HIDDEN INSTRUMENT**

Which musical instrument is hidden in the sentence below? Discover it by joining words or parts of words together.

WAS IT A REHEARSAL THAT WENT HORRIBLY WRONG THAT LED TO THE CONDUCTOR STEPPING DOWN?

302 **VOWEL PLAY**

The name of a ballet is shown without its vowels. Can you identify it?

R M N D J L T

(Three words)

303 **CYMBALISM**

Individual letters have been replaced by symbols. The first row names an instrument, the second a Spanish dance, the third a composer and the fourth a musical term.

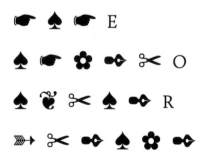

304 **OCTET**

Solve the clues below to find the eight-letter answers. The first letter of the answer goes in the numbered square, and the answer can go clockwise or anticlockwise. You must work out which direction it goes.

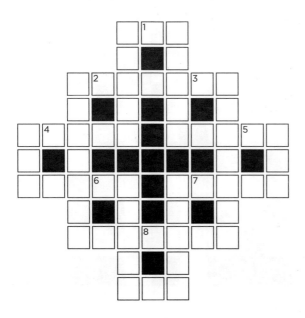

Clues

1   A Verdi opera and a Shakespeare character
2   Chinese pianist (4,4)
3   Performers who sing or play alone
4   Lighter musical work such as Lehár's *The Merry Widow*
5   The highest female voices
6   Keyboard player
7   Australian-born composer who has a museum named after him in Melbourne
8   Composer of the one-act *Cavalleria Rusticana*

305 **ENIGMA VARIATIONS**

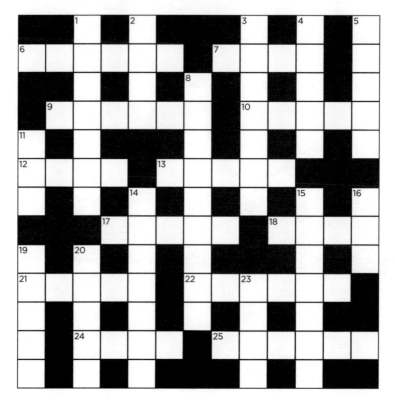

A cryptic crossword.

Across

6 Sounds as though this soprano might be insensitive (6)

7 A gal confused at the celebratory performance (4)

9 Frank composer with some span (6)

10 Bella reveals the record company's logo (5)

12 Provide aid a singer needs to perform this (4)

13 Throw the quality of sound on the scale (5)

17 Exotic dance from Tonga (5)

18 Sounds a very comfortable start to Mozart masterpiece (4)

21 Prolific composer, certainly no sloth! (5)

22 Performer with a variety of traits (6)

24 Beat this new item (4)

25 This girl certainly knows how to start singing praises! (6)

Down

1 Ilford a different place from Delius's orange grove (7)

2 The group suppressed, we hear (4)

3 This William was a braveheart according to Horner's music (7)

4 Sam balances carefully in this dance (5)

5 Ring at the end of the cell has strings (5)

8 Shostakovich symphony plans to land Reg in St Petersburg (9)

11 Devotee may keep cool with this (3)

14 Maigret unearths this type of music (7)

15 Harmonise with Albert or Philip? (7)

16 Ventilation melody (3)

19 Continuous echo irritates group of singers (5)

20 Not the Sharps in these high-rise blocks (5)

23 Narrate Rossini piece (4)

306 **NUMBER NAMES**

Each letter has been given a numerical value from 1 to 6. The total value of each word is reached by adding up the individual letters. No two letters have the same number.

T A L E S = 15

L I S T = 16

T I T L E = 17

S E A T S = 19

S A T I E = 20

What is the value of

T A L L I S ?

307 **TYPO**

Someone has made a mistake when preparing the programme for a concert. It's only one wrong letter, but it creates a new word and gives the title of the piece a whole new meaning! From the clue, can you identify the well-known work as it appears in the programme?

Clue
A sad-faced sweet girl features in a dream sequence from a cracker of a ballet.

308 **RING CYCLE**

Solve the clues below, which are in no particular order, and slot the seven-letter answers into their correct places in the ring. The last letter of one answer forms the first letter of the next. Answer 1 begins with the letter I.

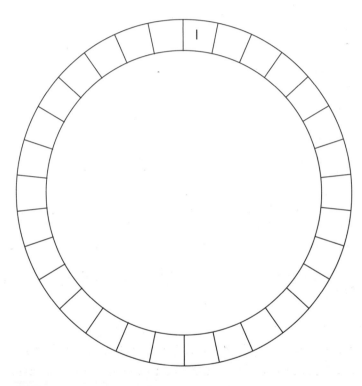

Clues

His work *William Tell* is widely regarded as his masterpiece
Travelling from venue to venue with a musical repertoire
High part added to the melody of a hymn or carol
Country that was the birthplace of flautist James Galway
Composer who wrote *The Moon and Sixpence* in 1957

309 **PHONOGRAPH**

Rearrange the letters to find the title of a long-established favourite from the concert repertoire. There are two words in the title.

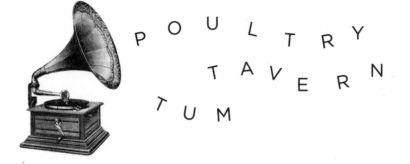

P O U L T R Y

T A V E R N

T U M

310 **I WAS THERE**

Look at the world event below and the names of the three composers. Using your knowledge of when the composers lived, which of them could have said, 'I was there'?

ALCOCK AND BROWN FLEW ACROSS THE ATLANTIC

Engelbert Humperdinck
Hubert Parry
Nikolai Rimsky-Korsakov

311 **MISSING VOICES**

The voices are soprano, alto, tenor and bass. The letters S, A, T and B (or some of these letters) are missing in the words below. Can you identify the 'missing voice' letters to find the name of the work?

?? CECILI? M???

312 **FIVE FIT**

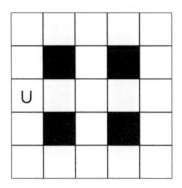

Solve the musical clues below, which are listed at random (all the answers contain five letters). Fit the answers into the grid, going either across or down. There is a starter letter to help you on your way.

Clues

Large brass instruments
Guitarist and lutenist Julian
This is played at a reveille in the armed forces
Play casually on a keyboard or guitar
No. 1 is this digit in piano playing fingering
Composer Jay, who wrote the *Ashokan Farewell*

313 **FILLERS**

Here are three words with the same letters missing. Find a single music-linked word to complete the longer words.

E V A _ _ _ E

R E S _ _ _ D

B A R B E _ _ _

314 **PRESTO**

A classic quick crossword.

Across

6 Romantic art songs such as those by Schubert or Strauss (6)

7 Bird native to the country Dame Kiri te Kanawa hails from (4)

9 Liverpool-born conductor who became Principal Conductor of the City of Birmingham Symphony Orchestra in 1979 (6)

10 Sir Peter, who created the role of *Peter Grimes* at Sadler's Wells in 1945 (5)

12 First name of composer Coates (4)

13 20th-century prime minister who installed a piano at No. 10 Downing Street (5)

17 Ponchielli's ballet, *Dance of the* _ _ _ _ _ (5)

18 Principal, courageous male character in an opera (4)

21 Finnish conductor (5)

22 Tenor Roberto who made his Royal Opera House debut in 1992 (6)

24 Vivacity, energy, fire! (4)

25 Hungarian composer who left Europe for New York in 1940 (6)

Down

1 French composer Iannis, of Greek parentage and Romanian birth (7)

2 The _ _ _ _ Eastern Divan Orchestra, is made up largely of musicians from the Middle East (4)

3 Composer of *The Mask of Time* (7)

4 Home of La Scala (5)

5 Five-act Gounod opera (5)

8 Practice for a performance (9)

11 Ralph Vaughan Williams, Symphony No, 1: *A* _ _ _ *Symphony* (3)

14 Russian composer Alexander, who was born and died in St Petersburg and composed mainly in his spare time (7)

15 English composer and pianist Sir Richard Rodney (7)

16 Part of Beethoven's Ninth, *Ode to* _ _ _ (3)

19 Sir Georg, Hungarian-born British conductor (5)

20 A Brazilian dance of African origin (5)

23 French composer Adolphe best known for the ballet *Giselle* (4)

315 WHAT AM I?

My first is in PHRASE
But isn't in HARP.
My second's in START
But isn't in SHARP.
My third is in PLAY
And also REHEARSE.
My fourth is in VIOL
Again it's in VERSE.
My fifth is in TEXT
And also in QUOTES.
I keep to straight lines
And jot down the notes.

316 FAST FORWARD

There are two clues to help you find two solutions. The first clue
leads you to a general word. The second clue leads you to a music-
based word. The solutions are very similar, but in the second word
the middle letter has moved *forwards* in the alphabet.

NIP

HIGH OR LOW NOTE SOUNDS

317 MOVIE A TO Z

Here is the name of a movie with music that has featured in the Classic FM Hall of Fame – but the letters are shown in alphabetical order. Rearrange the letters to find a three-word movie title.

A E E H H I K N N P P R T T

318 DIMINUENDO

Here are three clues to the identity of a famous composer. The number of points you earn diminishes the more clues you use. You earn THREE points if you only use Clue 1, TWO points if you need Clue 2, and just ONE point if you need Clue 3 as well.

Clue 1: This composer was reputedly Hitler's favourite composer, even though his wife was Jewish.

Clue 2: He was a pioneer of merchandising, with sales of hats, cigarettes and cocktails.

Clue 3: There were 778 performances in London of his famous *The Merry Widow*. King Edward VII saw four of them.

319 TRANSPOSED

Eccentric composer Ivor Song loves to apply strict patterns in his work. His music is full of modulations and melody lines that transpose from key to key, but the range between notes always remains constant. He has a favourite musical instrument that he has personalized by calling it FERNS. What type of instrument is it?

320 **MUSIC BOX**

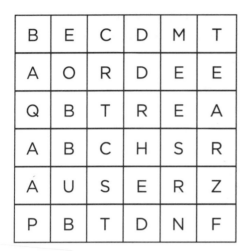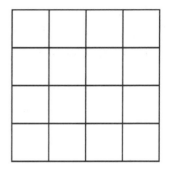

In a word square, the same words can be read either across or down. Your challenge is to make a word square in the empty grid. Three of the four words you need are hiding in the letter box, each one in a straight line that can go in any direction. The fourth word is the name of a musical instrument – you must decide which one!

321 **BACH-WORDS**

The name of a composer is hidden in the sentence below, but it has been written backwards. Look for a continuous line of letters from right to left to spell out the name.

AT THE SUCCESSFUL CONCERT THE OVERJOYED MEMBERS OF THE ORCHESTRA GLEEFULLY PLAYED YET ANOTHER ENCORE.

322 **HEXACHORD**

All answers have six letters. They can be written in the grid either clockwise or anticlockwise around the clue number. The first letter of Clue 1 is in place.

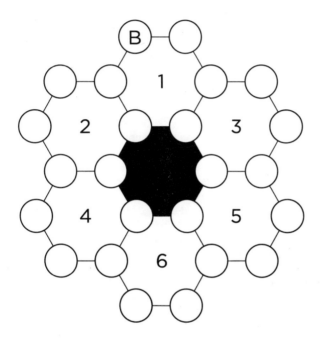

Clues

1   In the Victorian era, name given to any sentimental song
2   Instruction to play a piece leisurely and at ease
3   The seats in a theatre that are at ground level
4   The name given to groups of singers
5   The title of a Verdi song: 'Chorus of the Hebrew _ _ _ _ _ _'
6   Word meaning to set in motion a career or record label

323 BACK TO SCHOOL MUSIC QUIZ

We've designed another music quiz for children. If you get all the answers right, reward yourself with a gold star.

1 How would you best describe a minuet?
a)   A dance in 2/4 time
b)   A couple's dance
c)   A slow dance

2 What kind of instrument is a cornet?
a)   A brass instrument, like a baby trumpet
b)   A woodwind instrument, similar to an oboe
c)   A percussion instrument, used mainly in Renaissance music

3 Which musical instrument consists of a hoop with metal discs inserted around its frame, is held and shaken with one hand, while striking with the other?
a)   Cymbal
b)   Hoop drum
c)   Tambourine

4 In Tchaikovsky's *Swan Lake*, Princess Odette is turned into a swan. What is the only way for the spell to be broken?
a)   If her true love promises to marry her and also live as a swan
b)   If someone who has never loved before swears an oath of undying love
c)   If Odette receives true love's kiss by midnight

5 By what name is Beethoven's Bagatelle No. 25 in A minor better known?
a)   'Moonlight Sonata'
b)   'Ode to Joy'
c)   'Für Elise'

324 BACK TRACK

There are two clues to help you find two solutions. The first clue leads you to a general word. The second clue leads you to a music-based word. The solutions are very similar, but in the second word the middle letter has moved *backwards* in the alphabet.

PART OF A FLOWER

FOOT CONTROL ON A PIANO OR ORGAN

325 SPIRAL

```
┌───┬───┬───┬───┬───┬───┐
│ 1 │   │   │   │   │ 2 │
├───┼───┼───┼───┼───┼───┤
│   │   │ 6 │   │   │   │
├───┼───┼───┼───┼───┼───┤
│   │   │ 8 │   │   │   │
├───┼───┼───┼───┼───┼───┤
│   │   │   │   │   │ 3 │
├───┼───┼───┼───┼───┼───┤
│ 5 │   │ 7 │   │   │   │
├───┼───┼───┼───┼───┼───┤
│   │ 4 │   │   │   │   │
└───┴───┴───┴───┴───┴───┘
```

Solve the clues and write your answers in a clockwise direction in the spiral grid. Each answer begins in a numbered space. The words overlap each other in the spiral, with at least the last letter of one answer becoming the first letter of the next.

Clues
1   Small woodwind instrument
2   Soprano Dame Felicity
3   Opera where 'Nessun Dorma' is heard
4   Mezzo soprano Anne Sofie von _____
5   Welsh baritone Bryn
6   Librettist
7   Austrian family who popularised the waltz
8   'Where Corals Lie' is part of Elgar's _____ Pictures

326 NINTH SYMPHONY

Each number from 1 to 9 represents a different letter of the alphabet. Solve the clues and write the letters in the correct spaces in the grid to reveal a music-related word or name.

1	2	3	4	5	6	7	8	9

Clues

a) A soprano or a contralto   124398
b) A melody   6749
c) Indian musical instrument   12658

327 FORTUNE TELLER

The fortune teller can see into the future. Whose fortune is she telling here?

'You will become one of Russia's leading scientists and the Professor of Chemistry at the St Petersburg Academy of Medicine.

'You will be one of The Five, a group of nationalist composers, which will include Rimsky-Korsakov and Modest Mussorgsky.

'The musical *Kismet* will be based on the theme of the Nocturne from your String Quartet No. 2.'

328 **PERFECT FIFTH**

Solve the clues, which are listed at random. Each answer contains five letters. Complete the grid so that each answer starts in a space with an odd number and ends in the space with the even number that is one greater. To give you a perfect start, the letter in space 1 is M.

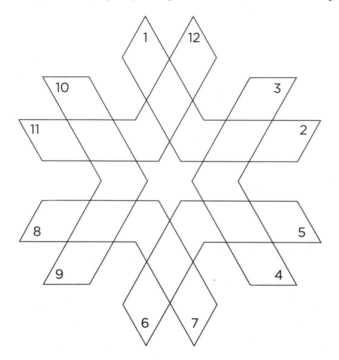

Clues

All in, this month in spring in the evening
Key for someone under the age of 18
March King, also, USA composer
Champagne glass in the woodwind section
Palms sway with church song
Dance moves up a ladder?

329 **THE LOST CHORD**

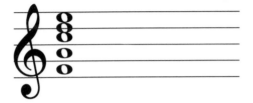

In a stave in the treble clef, the notes reading upwards in the spaces are F, A, C and E. The notes reading upwards on the lines are E, G, B, D and F. The sequence continues with notes above and below the stave.

Our stave shows a chord that has lost one note. The clue below leads to an answer made up of the letters of the notes shown in the stave, with an extra letter, A to G.

Can you find the missing note to complete the lost chord?

Clue
Front of a building made in the 1920s.

330 **REARRANGEMENT**

There are two clues to help you find two solutions. The first clue leads you to a general word. The second clue leads you to a music-based word. You will need all your skills as an arranger, as the second word is an anagram of the first – it has all the same letters, but in a different order.

COOKING IN AN OVEN

KEYBOARD MUSICIAN

331 NUMBER NAMES

Each letter has been given a numerical value from 1 to 6. The total value of each word is reached by adding up the individual letters. No two letters have the same number.

L I E D = 10

E L F = 11

O D E = 12

F I D D L E = 20

What is the value of

F I D E L I O ?

332 MISSING VOICES

The voices are soprano, alto, tenor and bass. The letters S, A, T and B (or some of these letters) are missing in the words below. Can you identify the 'missing voice' letters to find the name of the work?

? ? M ? O N

333 ADDERS

Find two answers that can be added together to form a new word with a musical link.

What do you get if you add being able to, to a word of parting?

334 THE CLASSICAL MUSICAL PUB QUIZ

Do you have an encyclopaedic knowledge of music trivia? Test yourself by answering these classical music questions.

1 What subtitle goes with Gilbert and Sullivan's operetta *The Pirates of Penzance*?
a)   The Witch's Curse
b)   The Lass that Loved a Sailor
c)   The Slave of Duty
d)   The Peer and the Peri

2 Which composer wrote two piano concertos, one violin concerto and one double concerto for violin and cello?
a)   Beethoven
b)   Brahms
c)   Bach
d)   Bruch

3 In which country was Delibes' opera *Lakmé* set?
a)   Sri Lanka
b)   Myanmar
c)   India
d)   Vietnam

4 Which of these vehicles did Herbert von Karajan *not* appear with on the cover of one of his recordings?
a)   Aeroplane
b)   Boat
c)   Racing car
d)   Hovercraft

5 How many *Ballades* did Chopin write?
a)   4
b)   12
c)   24
d)   48

335 **NAME CHECK**

Look at the clues below, which are in no particular order. Write the answer to each clue horizontally in the grid. You need to work out the correct order so that the shaded columns reveal the first name and surname of an English pianist.

1				
2				
3				
4				

Clues
White flower, which often grows on lawns
Wheel coverings
Frozen dew
City in Nebraska on the Missouri river

336 **ALPHA MALE**

The letters below make up the name of a male singer, but they are presented in alphabetical order. Rearrange the letters to reveal the singer's identity.

A C C E I N O O R R S U

337 **METRONOME**

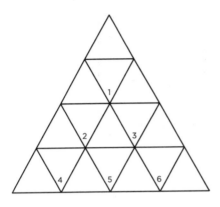

Each answer contains four letters. The first letter goes in a numbered triangle, the second letter directly above it, the third letter to the right and the fourth to the left.

Clues

1 Weather forecast for Madame Butterfly?
2 Producer of travelling opera, Ellen
3 Sign of the unknown composer
4 College with a famous boating song
5 Sondheim musical, _ _ _ _ *the Woods*
6 Sousa march *The Washington* _ _ _ _

338 **SPLIT PERSONALITY**

The letters in a composer's name have been split and rearranged. The composer's first name and surname both have seven letters. The letters in each name remain in the correct order. Who is the composer?

F P R O A U N L E C N I S C

339 **SUDO-KEY**

mn			C		mj			D
		C				A		
F			E		A			B
	E						C	
	F	mj		C		E	G	
D				A				mj
	D	G		B		F	A	
	mn						D	
C				E				G

In this puzzle, each block of nine squares must contain the letters of the keys A, B, C, D, E, F and G, along with mj to denote a major key and mn to denote a minor key. Every row (going across) and every column (going down) must contain nine different keys.

340 **FILLERS**

Here are three words with the same letters missing. Find a single music-linked word to complete the longer words.

B _ _ _ _ I N G

G _ _ _ _ I N E S S

F _ _ _ _ O M

341 **FORTUNE TELLER**

The fortune teller can see into the future. Whose fortune is she telling here?

'Although you will become well known as a composer in your native USA and abroad, you will also be a talented baritone singer.

'Your *Adagio for Strings* will be conducted by Toscanini in 1938, after which you will go from strength to strength.

'The *Adagio* will be played at the funerals of two American presidents, Roosevelt and Kennedy, and that of Princess Grace of Monaco.'

342 ANOTHER QUIZ FOR CLASSICAL MUSIC EXPERTS

This music theory test has been expertly designed to be an absolute head-scratcher, and it's not for the faint-hearted. Proceed with caution...

1 The traditional song 'Scarborough Fair' is based on which musical mode?
a)   Dorian
b)   Lydian
c)   Mixolydian
d)   Phrygian

2 What is the relative major of G minor?
a)   C major
b)   A flat major
c)   B flat major
d)   F major

3 Spot the fake Italian musical term...
a)   Coda
b)   Farsa
c)   Appendiabiti
d)   Mosso

4 Fill in the gap: the oboe has a range of approximately _____ octaves.
a)   Two and a half
b)   One and a half
c)   Three and a half
d)   Two

5 What is the Italian performance direction for 'touched'?
a)   Toccata
b)   Tenuto
c)   Tranquillo
d)   Tutti

343 FILLERS

Here are three words with the same letters missing. Find a single music-linked word to complete the longer words.

_ _ _ R I S T E R

G A _ _ _ D I N E

E M _ _ _ R A S S

344 THE CLASSICAL MUSIC REVISION QUIZ

Do you know literally everything there is to know about classical music? Or do you need to go back to music college? Dust off the textbooks and find out your result.

1 The better-known name of Beethoven's Third Symphony is...
a)   Choral
b)   Fate
c)   Pastoral
d)   Eroica

2 The tone poem for orchestra 'Dance Macabre' was written by which composer?
a)   Debussy
b)   Massenet
c)   Saint-Saëns
d)   Fauré

3 This fish's skin was used to sand violins during the 18th century. (No we're not joking.)
a)   Fangtooth
b)   Dogfish
c)   Boxfish
d)   Piranha

4 One of the most famous operettas is *Die Fledermaus*. What does the title mean?
a)   The Bat
b)   The Ugly Duckling
c)   The Tragedy of Count Fleder
d)   The Sly Mouse

5 The length of time Bach spent in jail for quitting his job was...
a)   3 days
b)   13 days
c)   30 days
d)   300 days

345 ADDERS

Find two answers that can be added together to form a new word with a musical link.

What do you get if you add a trick-taking card game to a French word for 'the'?

346 **HEXACHORD**

All answers have six letters. They can be written in the grid either clockwise or anticlockwise around the clue number. The first letter of Clue 1 is in place.

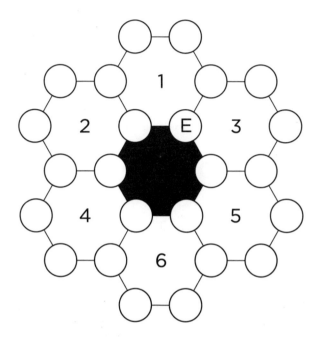

Clues

1   Mendelssohn oratorio about an Old Testament prophet
2   Musician whose ragtime music was used in the movie *The Sting*
3   Name given to a choral setting of a religious text
4   Another word for a stage or dais
5   Composer whose Eighth Symphony is called the *Symphony of a Thousand*
6   Surname of German violinist Anne Sophie

347 **HIDDEN INSTRUMENT**

Which musical instrument is hidden in the sentence below?
Discover it by joining words or parts of words together.

HE FAILED TO TURN UP FOR A PRACTICE
SESSION, BUT UNDER THE CIRCUMSTANCES
WE HOPE THEY DON'T BAN JOHN FROM THE
PERFORMANCE ITSELF.

348 **FAST FORWARD**

There are two clues to help you find two solutions. The first clue
leads you to a general word. The second clue leads you to a music-
based word. The solutions are very similar, but in the second word
the middle letter has moved *forwards* in the alphabet.

SMALL MEASURES OF SPIRITS

PERCUSSION INSTRUMENTS

349 SESTET

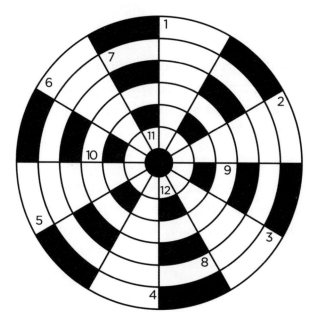

All answers have six letters. 1 to 6 start in the outer circle and are written towards the centre. 7 to 12 go around the rings in a clockwise direction.

Clues

1   Country in which Rachmaninov was born
2   Verdi opera loosely based on a Shakespeare play
3   A berceuse is also sometimes called this type of song
4   City in which Dvořák died in 1904
5   Another name for the windpipe – vital for singers
6   Another word for to originate, to make from scratch
7   Instrument associated with Julian Bream and John Williams
8   First name of the American/Polish composer Rubinstein
9   Music term meaning 'in slow time'
10   In *Idomeneo*, the character Ilia is sometimes described as a '_ _ _ _ _ _ in distress'
11   Richard Strauss opera about a biblical character, based on a play by Oscar Wilde
12   Kitchen equipment that precedes drum in the name of a percussion instrument

350 **THE SINGING OPTOMETRIST**

Seymore Anmore is an optometrist who is a leading singer with the Thespian Operatic and Dramatic Society (TOADS).

Fresh from playing KOKO in Gilbert and Sullivan's *The Mikado*, he appeared as HOOK in a recent Christmas production. He has featured twice in the comic opera by Burnard and Sullivan singing the roles of both COX and BOX.

Seymore is very particular about the roles that he auditions for. Apart from an inflated ego and a misplaced belief that people enjoy his over-loud and under-accurate baritone voice, there is a very reasoned and consistent viewpoint that makes him look at those named characters. What is that viewpoint?

351 **BACK TRACK**

There are two clues to help you find two solutions. The first clue leads you to a general word. The second clue leads you to a music-based word. The solutions are very similar, but in the second word the middle letter has moved *backwards* in the alphabet.

CHANGE A BUILDING TO SERVE A NEW PURPOSE

MUSICAL PERFORMANCE COMPRISING SEVERAL SEPARATE PIECES

352 A BONUS MUSIC TRIVIA QUIZ

Put your skills to the test with these classical music brainteasers.
Can you get full marks?

1 To which insect did Rimsky-Korsakov dedicate his famous orchestral interlude?
a)   A bumblebee
b)   A wasp
c)   A grasshopper

2 Everyone knows the opera aria that goes 'Figaro, Figaro, Figaro'. Name that opera.
a)   *The Marriage of Figaro* (Mozart)
b)   *Don Giovanni* (Mozart)
c)   *The Barber of Seville* (Rossini)
d)   *Rigoletto* (Verdi)

3 Who was the composer best known for playing practical jokes?
a)   Wagner
b)   Liszt
c)   Haydn
d)   Vivaldi

4 George Walker is remembered for being...
a)   The first African American to win a Pulitzer Prize for Music
b)   The inventor of the piano
c)   The first Black musician to compose in court

5 Who invented the 12-tone system?
a)   Schoenberg
b)   Berg
c)   Steve Reich

353 MOVIE A TO Z

Here is the name of a movie with music that has featured in the
Classic FM Hall of Fame – but the letters are shown in alphabetical
order. Rearrange the letters to find a three-word movie title.

A C E F F H I I O O R R S T

354 **DIMINUENDO**

Here are three clues to the identity of a famous composer. The number of points you earn diminishes the more clues you use. You earn THREE points if you only use Clue 1, TWO points if you need Clue 2, and just ONE point if you need Clue 3 as well.

Clue 1: This composer played the first English performance of Beethoven's *Emperor Concerto*.

Clue 2: He taught piano to Prince Albert, and dedicated his *Scottish Symphony* to Queen Victoria and her husband.

Clue 3: His ever popular 'Wedding March' comes from *A Midsummer Night's Dream*.

355 **I WAS THERE**

Look at the world event below and the names of the three composers. Using your knowledge of when the composers lived, which of them could have said, 'I was there'?

THE CORONATION OF QUEEN ELIZABETH II

Sergei Prokofiev
Ralph Vaughan Williams
Kurt Weill

356 **MISSING VOICES**

The voices are soprano, alto, tenor and bass. The letters S, A, T and B (or some of these letters) are missing in the words below. Can you identify the 'missing voice' letters to find the name of the work?

E X ? U L ? ? ? E,   J U ? I L ? ? E

357 OCTET

Solve the clues below to find the eight-letter answers. The first letter of the answer goes in the numbered square, and the answer can go clockwise or anticlockwise. You must work out which direction it goes.

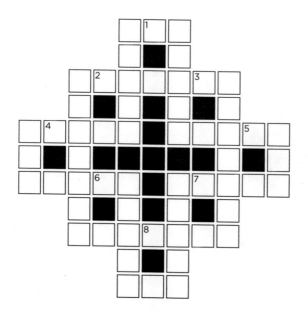

Clues

1 Finnish patriot famous for *Finlandia*
2 Professional entertainer of the 12th to the 17th centuries
3 Orchestral introduction to an opera
4 Estonian who won a prize for his children's cantata *Our Garden* (4,4)
5 19th-century Austrian organist who felt his *Te Deum* was one of his greatest works
6 Piece where a solo instrument contrasts with an orchestral ensemble
7 20th-century French composer who wrote an opera on the life of St Francis of Assisi
8 Brass instruments

358 **HEXACHORD**

All answers have six letters. They can be written in the grid either
clockwise or anticlockwise around the clue number. The first letter
of Clue 1 is in place.

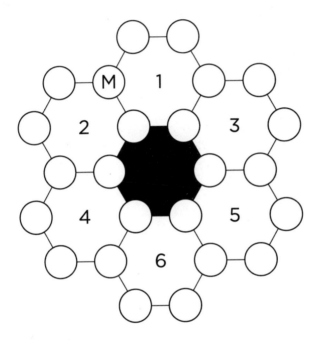

Clues

1 Composer of *Eine Kleine Nachtmusik*
2 Mussorgsky's unassuming first name
3 English composer Malcolm, who wrote the scores for around 100 films
4 Subdivisions of acts
5 City where you will find the Wigmore Hall
6 Traditional name for Christmas hymns and songs

359 QUICK QUOTE

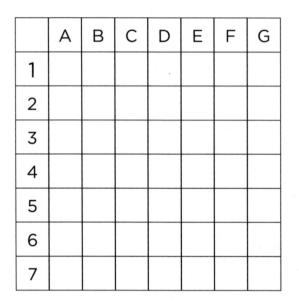

Solve the quick clues and write your answers across in the grid.

Clues

1   Handel's country of birth
2   Language he used when writing in Rome
3   Famous works, *The Coronation* _____
4   A flourish from the instruments in 7 used for ceremonial purposes
5   Subject of an oratorio about an Old Testament wise man
6   An oratorio included the 'Hallelujah Chorus'
7   Brass instrument used by Handel in obbligatos

Now, using the grid references (A1, B5, etc.), take the letter from the space indicated and write it below to reveal a quotation. This is from a newspaper following the first performance of Handel's *Royal Fireworks*. The quotation starts to describe it as 'a grand whim...'. How does the quotation finish?

A4.F5.C1   E7.B5.C6.B2.E3.F4.E2.A7.G1   C3.D5   D2.E1.C7.A1.G6   E4.G7

_____   _____   _____   _____   _____

360 **NOTATION**

Each letter that appears in the treble clef (A, B, C, D, E, F and G) has been replaced by a musical note. The other letters of the alphabet are in place. Can you work out the name of the composer and a piece of their music?

H ♪ N ♪♪ L

S ♪ R ♪♪♪ N ♪♪

361 **CYMBALISM**

Individual letters have been replaced by symbols. The first row names an instrument, the second a dance, the third composer and the fourth a musical term.

362 WHAT AM I?

My first is in CLAP
But isn't in PLAY.
My second's in DANCE
And also in SWAY.
My third is in ARIA
And also in ART.
My fourth is in STOP
But isn't in START.
My fifth's in LEHÁR
But isn't in HEAR.
My tune and my words
Feature every year.

363 NUMBER SUM

Test your musical knowledge and your skill in basic arithmetic in one puzzle.

Multiply the number of Beethoven symphonies by the number of days of Christmas in the traditional song.

364 GUESS THE CHRISTMAS CAROL

We've put together a set of emoji clues for some well-known Christmas carols – some a little more cryptic than others. Can you figure out the answers?

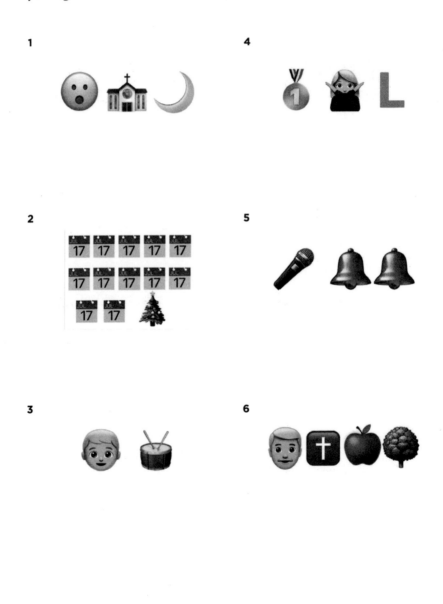

1

2

3

4

5

6

7

10

8

11

9

12

365 CHRISTMAS CAROL LYRICS QUIZ

You know 'Herod the King, in his raging...'. But how many other Christmas carol lyrics can you get right? Don your antlers, dust off your 'Carols for Choirs' book, and let's go...

1 Good King Wenceslas looked out
a)   On the Feast of Stephen
b)   Yonder East of Stephen
c)   On the Eve of Christmas
d)   Early Christmas morning

2 The first Nowell, the angel did say
a)   That a certain poor shepherd lay deep in the hay
b)   On a cold winter's night in fields as they say
c)   Was to certain poor shepherds in fields as they lay
d)   A star drew nigh in the cold winter's hay

3 For happiness I long have sought
a)   By faith I know, but ne'er can tell
b)   And pleasure dearly I have bought
c)   With all the fish I could have caught
d)   Which makes my soul in haste to be

4 We three kings of Orient are
a)   Guide us to the yonder star
b)   Westward leading, still proceeding
c)   Following the yonder star
d)   Bearing gifts we traverse afar

5 O Jesu parvule,
a)   O Hear me, I beseech Thee
b)   From Thee I turn away
c)   For Thee I yearn away
d)   All joy to Thee I pray

6 Oh sisters two, how may we do
a)   For to preserve this day
b)   Forever mourn and say
c)   I can their far venture, stay
d)   Dream now, lully, lullay

7 He came down to Earth from heaven,
a)   And His cradle was a stall
b)   And he leads his children on
c)   Who is God and Lord of all
d)   All in white shall wait around

8 The stars in the bright sky look down where He lay,
a)   The little Lord Jesus asleep on the hay
b)   But Little Lord Jesus no crying he makes
c)   Be near me Lord Jesus, I ask Thee to stay
d)   Stay by me forever and love me, I pray

9 While mortals sleep, the angels keep
a)   The silent stars go by
b)   Their watch of wondering love
c)   The wondrous gift of heav'n
d)   Thy deep and dreamless sleep

10 God of God, Light of Light
a)   Lo, He abhors not the Virgin's womb
b)   Sing, all ye citizens of heaven above
c)   Jesus, to Thee be glory given
d)   Word of the Father, now in flesh appearing

11 Our God, heaven cannot hold Him
a)   Water like a stone
b)   Worship night and day
c)   Nor earth sustain
d)   When He comes to reign

SOLUTIONS

1 NOTATION

GRIEG
PEER GYNT

2 SPLIT PERSONALITY

JOHN CAGE

3 NUMBER SUM

'Minute Waltz' (60 seconds) x *The Three-Cornered Hat* = 180

4 HALF TIME

1   Fire
2   Read
3   Adam
4   Amen
5   Enya

5 CYMBALISM

HORN
HORNER
CORNET
ENCORE

6 METRONOME

1   Four
2   Fret
3   Rule
4   Otto
5   Beat
6   Elsa

7 THREE DIVAS

Dido wears: white dress, green shoes, black wrap
Lulu wears: black dress, white shoes, green wrap
Mimi wears: green dress, black shoes, white wrap

8 NUMBER NAMES

VIVALDI = 18
V = 1, I = 2, D = 3, A = 4, L = 5

9 OCTET

1   Schubert (C)
2   Serenade (C)
3   Dulcimer (A)
4   Violetta (A)
5   American (A)
6   Playlist (C)
7   Crotchet (C)
8   Rhapsody (C)

10 HIDDEN INSTRUMENT

CELLO

11 PHONOGRAPH

FINLANDIA (Sibelius)

12 MISSING VOICES

THE BARTERED BRIDE (Smetana)

13 SUDO-KEY

G	mn	C	mj	B	E	A	F	D
B	D	F	mn	C	A	mj	E	G
E	mj	A	D	G	F	C	mn	B
A	C	B	F	mn	mj	D	G	E
mn	E	G	C	D	B	F	mj	A
mj	F	D	E	A	G	B	C	mn
D	G	mj	B	E	C	mn	A	F
F	A	mn	G	mj	D	E	B	C
C	B	E	A	F	mn	G	D	mj

14 THE LOST CHORD

Note A is needed to make CAGE.
John Cage is a composer.
A cage is used to imprison, or pen, people or animals.

15 TYPO

The Barker of Seville
Barker should be *Barber.*

16 WHAT AM I?

BATON

17 **NOTATION**

GRAINGER
BRIGG FAIR

18 **THE QUIZ FOR CLASSICAL MUSIC FANS**

1   b) Chicken
2   c) 88
3   d) 1812
4   b) 4
5   b) £15 million

19 **HEXACHORD**

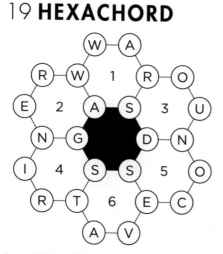

1   Warsaw (C)
2   Wagner (C)
3   Rounds (C)
4   String (C)
5   Second (A)
6   Staves (A)

20 RING CYCLE

1 Stainer
2 Requiem
3 Maestro
4 Ocarina
5 Anthems

21 SESTET

1 Andrew
2 Berlin
3 Callas
4 Goethe
5 Verses
6 Joshua
7 Angela
8 *Bolero*
9 Flutes
10 *Choral*
11 Twangs
12 Geisha

22 INVISIBLES

BAX

23 REARRANGEMENT

MIGRATE
RAGTIME

24 ADDERS

Canon

25 **VOWEL PLAY**

Metropolitan Opera House

26 **THE CLASSICAL MUSIC QUIZ DESIGNED FOR CHILDREN**

1   b) 20th century
2   False
3   c) Saxophone
4   a) Breve
5   b) F minor

27 **DIMINUENDO**

Antonín Dvořák

28 **PRESTO**

Across

6   Galway
7   Riga
9   Treble
10 Elder
12 Arne
13 Ungar
17 Sixth
18 Male
21 China
22 Imogen
24 Gods
25 Boston

Down

1   Clarino
2   Lamb
3   Wiseman
4   Haydn
5   Sharp
8   Bernstein
11 Bax
14 Vivaldi
15 Gabetta
16 Ben
19 Scott
20 Binge
23 Oboe

29 **FIVE FIT**

30 **MUSIC BOX**

WITH
IDEA
TEAR
HARP

31 **BACH-WORDS**

TALLIS

32 **SPIRAL**

1   Djawadi
2   Dietrich
3   Cha cha cha
4   Hallé
5   Leeds
6   *Seven*
7   Evening
8   Glad

33 CIRCLES

The question mark is the letter R.
Top left: Britten
Top right: *Gloriana*
Bottom: *Nocturne*

34 COMPOSING

1   POULENC
2   QUINTET
3   ENCORED
4   CONCERT
5   BERLIOZ
6   COPLAND
7   SALIERI
PUCCINI is formed in the shaded diagonal.

35 NAME CHECK

1   PHRASES
2   THISTLE
3   EXCERPT
4   UNHEARD
5   GRADUAL
6   PARASOL
7   MODESTY
RICHARD STRAUSS

36 NINTH SYMPHONY

a)   BASSOON
b)   ARIA
c)   NOTE
BARITONES

37 I WAS THERE

GUSTAV HOLST (1874–1934)
Puccini died in 1924.
Janáček died in 1928.
The first football World Cup was in 1930.

38 TYPO

Fingal's Rave
Rave should be *Cave.*

39 BACK TRACK

GLOSS
GLASS

40 QUIZ CROSSWORD

Across

7 *Menace*
9 Adagio
10 Impresario
11 City
12 Bruch
13 Pachelbel
15 Puccini
20 *Mountains*
21 Savoy
23 Dido
24 *Prince Igor*
25 Rameau
26 Rodney

Down

1 Denmark
2 Maurice
3 Welsh
4 Saxophone
5 Malcolm
6 Sixties
8 *Lark Ascending*
14 Sugar plum
16 Bolivar
17 Encores
18 *Matilda*
19 Colonel
22 Score

41 **HALF TIME**

1   *Holy*
2   Lyre
3   Rest
4   Stop
5   Opus

42 **FAST FORWARD**

BIDET
BIZET

43 **RING CYCLE**

1   Antonio
2   Octaves
3   Sackbut
4   *Troilus*
5   Smetana

44 **WHAT'S THE LINK?**

1   Janacek
2   Mars
3   *Juliet*
4   Nocturne
All the answers contain abbreviations of calendar months (Jan, Mar, Jul and Oct).

45 **ALPHA MALE**

ALFIE BOE

46 CYMBALISM

LUTE
MUTTER
TRUMPET
REPEAT

47 THE TRICKY MUSIC THEORY TEST

1   a) Slowly
2   c) Baroque
3   d) Compound
4   b) Dying away
5   d) Crostini

48 MOVIE A TO Z

DANCES WITH WOLVES (John Barry)

49 PERFECT FIFTH

1   Album
3   Suite
5   Steel
7   Pears
9   Track
11   Scale

50 MISS HERD

CUE, BASE and BANNED need to change.
There is an enormous queue around the opera house. The bass singer is proving to be very popular with his band 'Ensemble'.

51 FORTUNE TELLER

George Frideric Handel

52 JOHN WILLIAMS WORD SEARCH

The film listed twice is *SCHINDLER'S LIST*.

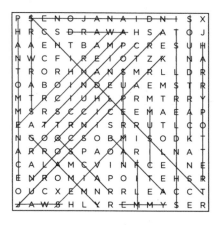

53 OCTET

1   *Pictures* (C)
2   Trombone (C)
3   Resonant (C)
4   Libretto (A)
5   Nocturne (A)
6   Massenet (C)
7   Lyricist (A)
8   Williams (C)

54 THE LOST CHORD

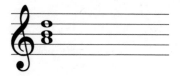

Note A is needed to make BAD.
Prokofiev wrote *Peter and The Wolf*.
The Disney depiction left no doubt about the character of the wolf!

55 **NUMBER SUM**

31 days (October) + 31 days (May) = 62

56 **METRONOME**

1   Moon
2   Snow
3   Como
4   Swan
5   Coda
6   Amid

57 **VOWEL PLAY**

Daphnis and Chloë (Ravel)

58 **THE QUIZ FOR MUSIC HISTORIANS**

1   b) 2
2   b) Ludwig van Beethoven
3   b) Glissando
4   c) Schubert
5   b) Haydn

59 **WHAT AM I?**

TUNE

60 ENIGMA VARIATIONS

Across

6 Guitar
7 Mega
9 Mahler
10 India
12 Asia
13 Child
17 Bliss
18 Lute
21 Score
22 Record
24 Mars
25 Cinema

Down

1 Titanic
2 Karl
3 Seville
4 Haydn
5 Bleak
8 Orchestra
11 Bax
14 Allegro
15 Quartet
16 Key
19 Psalm
20 *Norma*
23 Clip

61 QUICK QUOTE

1 Teacher
2 Norwich
3 William
4 Rhythms
5 Violins
6 *Chanson*
7 Malvern

Quotation: *Love alone shall stay.*

62 AS EASY AS ABC

1 Bach
2 Canteloube
3 Pachelbel

63 PHONOGRAPH

MOONLIGHT SONATA (Beethoven)

64 **HEXACHORD**

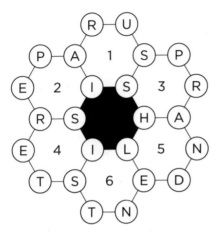

1   Russia (C)
2   Persia (A)
3   Sharps (A)
4   Sister (C)
5   Handel (C)
6   Silent (C)

65 **SESTET**

1   Hector
2   Joplin
3   Lyrics
4   Phrase
5   Greece
6   *Chorus*
7   Melody
8   Church
9   Finale
10   *Gretel*
11   Arenas
12   Aeneas

66 THE IMPOSSIBLE MUSIC TRIVIA QUIZ

1   c) The first American woman to compose and publish a symphony
2   c) 20
3   b) Peter Warlock
4   a) Léonin
5   c) In a fun, joyful manner

67 DIMINUENDO

George Gershwin (the piece in Clue 2 is *Rhapsody in Blue*)

68 SUDO-KEY

F	C	A	G	mn	E	mj	B	D
mj	E	B	F	A	D	mn	C	G
D	G	mn	C	mj	B	A	F	E
A	D	C	mj	E	F	B	G	mn
B	mn	E	D	C	G	F	A	mj
G	mj	F	A	B	mn	D	E	C
E	A	G	B	D	mj	C	mn	F
C	F	mj	mn	G	A	E	D	B
mn	B	D	E	F	C	G	mj	A

69 HIDDEN INSTRUMENT

PICCOLO

70 NOTATION

BACH
MAGNIFICAT

71 **ALPHA MALE**

MICHAEL BALL

72 **MUSIC BOX**

PLAY
LYRE
ARIA
YEAR

73 **SPLIT PERSONALITY**

FRANZ LEHÁR

74 **FIVE FIT**

75 **TYPO**

The Last Pose of Summer
Pose should be *Rose.*

76 **CIRCLES**

The question mark is the letter I.
Top left: *Lohengrin*
Top right: *Parsifal*
Bottom: *Siegfried*

77 **SPIRAL**

1   Anthem
2   Emma
3   Madrigal
4   Galway
5   Yuja
6   Jarecki
7   Kirov
8   Viola
9   Lament

78 **NUMBER NAMES**

RECORDER = 24
E = 1, D = 2, O = 3, R = 4, C = 5

79 **REARRANGEMENT**

GATES
STAGE

80 **INVISIBLES**

HOLST

81 **NAME CHECK**

1   ACTOR
2   CARRY
3   DRIFT
4   CLIFF
CARL ORFF

82 **FILLERS**

ARIA (VARIATIONS, PARIAH, MALARIA)

83 RING CYCLE

1   *Matthew*
2   Worship
3   Perahia
4   Austria
5   Anagram

84 FAST FORWARD

HOIST
HOLST

85 BACH-WORDS

WALTON

86 I WAS THERE

IGOR STRAVINSKY (1882–1971)
Grainger died in 1961.
Gershwin died in 1937.
The first successful heart transplant was in 1967.

87 THE HARDEST EVER CHILDREN'S MUSIC QUIZ

1   b) A piece of music in one movement, which paints an idea or theme
2   b) Cadenza
3   c) Pastoral
4   c) Music that's the same when played backwards as it is when it's played forwards
5   a) *Peter and the Wolf*

88 **HALF TIME**

1 Hifi
2 Fife
3 *Fear*
4 Aria
5 Iamb

89 **NINTH SYMPHONY**

a) LINES
b) CLARA
c) SATIE
CLARINETS

90 **MOVIE A TO Z**

LADIES IN LAVENDER (Nigel Hess)

91 **MUSICAL CONNECTIONS**

1 DRUM
2 ORGAN
3 WHISTLE
4 HORN
5 BELL

92 **BACK TRACK**

DUMAS
DUKAS

93 **REARRANGEMENT**

REPULSED
PRELUDES

94 THE MOST FIENDISH CLASSICAL MUSIC QUIZ EVER

1   c) Tragic
2   a) Variation XI (G.R.S.)
3   b) Oxford
4   b) Sir Malcolm Sargent
5   b) 60

95 PERFECT FIFTH

1   Pause
3   Oscar
5   Harps
7   Apple
9   Claps
11   Spear

96 NAME THE CLASSICAL MASTERPIECE FROM THE EMOJIS

1   *The Four Seasons* (Vivaldi)
2   'Wedding March' (Mendelssohn)
3   'Water Music' suite (Handel)
4   'Turkish March' (Mozart)
5   *The Planets* suite (Holst)
6   *The Nutcracker* (Tchaikovsky)
7   *Swan Lake* (Tchaikovsky)
8   *Pictures at an Exhibition* (Mussorgsky)
9   'Ode to Joy' (Beethoven)
10   *Night on the Bare Mountain* (Mussorgsky)
11   'New World Symphony' (Dvořák)
12   'The Lark Ascending' (Vaughan Williams)
13   'In the Hall of the Mountain King' (Grieg)
14   'Ghost' Trio (Beethoven)
15   'Flower Duet' (Delibes)
16   *The Firebird* (Stravinsky)
17   *Dance Macabre* (Saint-Saëns)
18   Dance of the Sugar Plum Fairy' (Tchaikovsky)
19   'Clair de lune' (Debussy)
20   *B minor mass* (Bach)
21   'A Boy and a Girl' (Whitacre)

97 MISS HERD

TENNER, BEAU and TUNA need to change.
The orchestra put out a plea for a tenor as they were a singer short. Fortunately the violinist collected her mislaid bow before the performance began. Worried about the pitch of her instrument the pianist was desperately trying to locate a tuner.

98 FORTUNE TELLER

Felix Mendelssohn

99 QUIZ CROSSWORD

Across

7 George
9 Etudes
10 Montserrat
11 Item
12 Miles
13 *Rigoletto*
15 Pleaser
20 Arabesque
21 Tenor
23 Mimi
24 *I Pagliacci*
25 Martha
26 Sonata

Down

1 Segovia
2 Britten
3 Peter
4 Beethoven
5 Jupiter
6 Celesta
8 *Carmina Burana*
14 Classical
16 *Arrival*
17 Oboists
18 Geraint
19 Toccata
22 Bliss

100 MATCH THE CLASSICAL COMPOSERS TO THEIR FIRST NAMES

1 c) Joseph
2 d) Sergei
3 a) Hildegard
4 c) Wolfgang
5 b) Antonio
6 c) Scott
7 d) Richard
8 b) Arnold
9 d) Maurice

101 **CYMBALISM**

BELL
BELLINI
BINGE
ELGAR

102 **VOWEL PLAY**

La Scala, Milan

103 **THE LOST CHORD**

Note D is needed to make DEAD.
Rachmaninov wrote *The Isle of the Dead*.

104 **MISSING VOICES**

ST MATTHEW PASSION (Bach)

105 **COMPOSING**

1   DELIBES
2   JENKINS
3   GIBBONS
4   NATURAL
5   PHRASES
6   REPRISE
7   HARMONY

DEBUSSY is formed in the shaded diagonal.

106 **SESTET**

1   Enrico
2   Gillam
3   Unison
4   Pascal
5   Saxony
6   Herald
7   Indian
8   Pavane
9   *Psycho*
10   Daniel
11   *Common*
12   Played

107 **OCTET**

1   Carl Orff (C)
2   Triangle (C)
3   Madrigal (C)
4   Folk song (A)
5   Oratorio (A)
6   Falsetto (C)
7   Staccato (C)
8   Bagpipes (C)

108 **MUSIC BOX**

FISH
INTO
STAR
HORN

109 **HIDDEN INSTRUMENT**

FLUTE

110 **COMPETITIVE**

1st = Sally
2nd = Tim
3rd = Viv
4th = Will

111 **NOTATION**

BINGE
ELIZABETHAN SERENADE

112 **FIVE FIT**

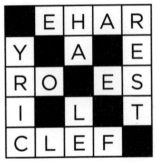

113 **TYPO**

YOUR TINY BAND IS FROZEN
BAND should be *HAND*.

114 **METRONOME**

1   *Isle*
2   Vere
3   Slur
4   Hess
5   Arts
6   *Hunt*

115 **ADDERS**

Fanfare

116 **SUDO-KEY**

mn	F	A	B	D	E	C	G	mj
C	D	E	F	G	mj	A	mn	B
B	G	mj	A	mn	C	E	F	D
D	E	B	C	F	A	G	mj	mn
G	mn	F	E	mj	D	B	C	A
mj	A	C	mn	B	G	F	D	E
E	B	mn	mj	C	F	D	A	G
F	mj	G	D	A	B	mn	E	C
A	C	D	G	E	mn	mj	B	F

117 **NUMBER SUM**

(1812) 1 + 8 + 1 + 2 = 12 + *Four Seasons* = 16

118 **SPLIT PERSONALITY**

ETHEL SMYTH

119 **PHONOGRAPH**

THE PEARL FISHERS (Bizet)

120 **PRESTO**

Across

6   Prévin
7   Duet
9   Rutter
10 Cello
12 Rush
13 Skill
17 Jonas
18 Mimi
21 Bliss
22 Ithaca
24 *Girl*
25 Patron

Down

1   Debussy
2   *List*
3   Purcell
4   Italy
5   Baton
8   Erik Satie
11 Ark
14 Consort
15 Discord
16 Jig
19 Ibsen
20 Wings
23 Hear

121 **LEADING LADIES WORD SEARCH**

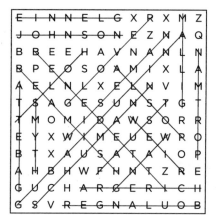

122 **INVISIBLES**

BRUCH

123 **WHAT AM I?**

SCALE

124 **FILLERS**

HUM (HUMIDITY, POSTHUMOUS, INHUMANE)

125 **RING CYCLE**

1   Copland
2   Delibes
3   Student
4   Trumpet
5   *Titanic*

126 **SPIRAL**

1   Mascagni
2   Ninth
3   Thieving
4   Gustavo
5   Vocalist
6   Stage
7   German

127 **HALF TIME**

1   Jota
2   Tape
3   Peer
4   Erda
5   Dawn

128 **DIMINUENDO**

Alexander Borodin

129 CIRCLES

The question mark is the letter O.
Top left: *The Mission*
Top right: Morricone
Bottom: Conductor

130 NUMBER NAMES

TOSCA = 19
T = 1, E = 2, O = 3, C = 4, S = 5, A = 6

131 BACH-WORDS

VERDI

132 NAME CHECK

1   HAPPY
2   BREAK
3   IVORY
4   FORTY
ARVO PÄRT

133 TYPO

THE FRYING DUTCHMAN
FRYING should be *FLYING*.

134 I WAS THERE

HENRY PURCELL (1659–95)
Gibbons died in 1625.
Monteverdi died in 1643.
The Great Fire of London was in 1666.

135 **MOVIE A TO Z**

DANGEROUS MOONLIGHT (Richard Addinsell)

136 **NINTH SYMPHONY**

a) BAKER
b) OBOES
c) DAY
KEYBOARDS

137 **ENIGMA VARIATIONS**

Across

6   Oberon
7   Deer
9   Bolero
10 Ivory
12 Aria
13 Alfie
17 Grand
18 Hero
21 Minim
22 Encore
24 Free
25 Venice

Down

1   Segovia
2   Joke
3   Cecilia
4   Arrow
5   Plays
8   Boulanger
11 Bad
14 Trumpet
15 Refrain
16 Low
19 Amble
20 Knife
23 Clef

138 **PERFECT FIFTH**

1   Tenor
3   Norma
5   Smyth
7   Stops
9   Spain
11 *Vixen*

139 'ODE TO JOY' OR THE US CONSTITUTION?

1   a) Ode to Joy
2   b) US Constitution
3   a) Ode to Joy
4   a) Ode to Joy
5   b) US Constitution
6   a) Ode to Joy
7   b) US Constitution
8   b) US Constitution
9   b) US Constitution

140 ALPHA MALE

ANDREA BOCELLI

141 FORTUNE TELLER

Giacomo Puccini

142 MISSING VOICES

COSÌ FAN TUTTE (Mozart)

143 MUSIC BOX

ROLL
OBOE
LOVE
LEEK

144 MUSICAL MENU

EGG
Dad always favours things whose names can be made from the musical scale A, B, C, D, E, F and G. So his favourite sandwich has to be egg.

145 **BACK TRACK**

FAYRE
FAURÉ

146 **FAST FORWARD**

GRAVES
GROVES

147 **QUICK QUOTE**

1   America
2   British
3   New York
4   Finales
5   Conduct
6   Bow/Duo
7   *Journey*

Quotation: *[Music] creates order out of chaos.*

148 **METRONOME**

1   Ball
2   Glee
3   *Blue*
4   *West*
5   Keys
6   *Jury*

149 **NUMBER SUM**

Four Last Songs x *Seven Years in Tibet* = 28

150 **SESTET**

1   Mahler
2   Jessye
3   *Juliet*
4   Jingle
5   Talent
6   Mozart
7   Rameau
8   *Mikado*
9   Single
10 Tallis
11 Priest
12 Septet

151 **FIVE FIT**

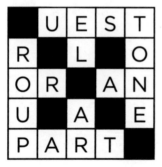

152 **HIDDEN INSTRUMENT**

DRUM

153 **THE LOST CHORD**

Note F is needed to make FEED.
The song 'Feed The Birds' featured in the movie *Mary Poppins*.

154 **CYMBALISM**

GONG
OGDON
GOUNOD
RODRIGO

155 **SPIRAL**

1   Reade
2   Delibes
3   Estonia
4   Anvil
5   Villa Lobos
6   Boston
7   *Onegin*
8   Neck

156 **CIRCLES**

The question mark is the letter A.
Top left: Albert
Top right: Festival
Bottom: Barbican

157 **OCTET**

1   Composer (C)
2   Chansons (A)
3   Applause (A)
4   Ensemble (C)
5   Quintets (A)
6   Whitacre (C)
7   Schumann (A)
8   *Turandot* (C)

158 **OPERA OR APPLE?**

1	Apple		13	Opera
2	Apple		14	Opera
3	Opera		15	Apple
4	Apple		16	Apple
5	Opera		17	Apple
6	Apple		18	Opera
7	Opera		19	Apple
8	Opera		20	Apple
9	Apple		21	Opera
10	Apple		22	Apple
11	Opera		23	Apple
12	Apple			

159 **VOWEL PLAY**

Beauty and the Beast (Tchaikovsky)

160 **PERFECT FIFTH**

1	Start
3	Trios
5	Yodel
7	Pedal
9	Hands
11	Edits

161 **INVISIBLES**

XENAKIS

162 **ADDERS**

Concert

163 **HALF TIME**

1   Loki
2   Kiri
3   Ride
4   Deal
5   Aled

164 **NOTATION**

EINAUDI
LE ONDE

165 **SUDO-KEY**

C	E	A	F	D	mj	G	B	mn
G	B	D	mn	A	C	mj	F	E
F	mn	mj	G	B	E	D	A	C
D	F	E	B	mj	mn	C	G	A
mn	G	C	D	E	A	B	mj	F
mj	A	B	C	G	F	E	mn	D
A	mj	G	E	F	D	mn	C	B
B	D	mn	A	C	G	F	E	mj
E	C	F	mj	mn	B	A	D	G

166 **REARRANGEMENT**

REIGNS
SINGER

167 **DIMINUENDO**

Frederick Delius

168 **SALE PRICE**

The sale price was £1,875.
The cello was on sale for £2,500. It went for 75% of that price.

169 **PHONOGRAPH**

THE MAGIC FLUTE (Mozart)

170 **A CLASSICAL MUSIC GENERAL KNOWLEDGE CHALLENGE**

1   d) Simon Callow
2   a) Carthage
3   c) 1973
4   b) Sir Walter Parratt
5   d) Madonna

171 **NINTH SYMPHONY**

a)   CHOIRS
b)   MINIM
c)   MARCH
HARMONICS

172 **NUMBER NAMES**

ROCOCO = 20
O = 1, N = 2 or 3, T = 2 or 3, E = 4, R = 5, C = 6

173 **SPLIT PERSONALITY**

FRANZ LISZT

174 **FILLERS**

VIOL (NONVIOLENCE, RAVIOLI, VIOLETS)

175 **BACH-WORDS**

ORFF

176 **HEXACHORD**

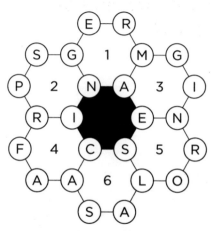

1   German (C)
2   *Spring* (A)
3   *Enigma* (A)
4   *Africa* (C)
5   Enrols (C)
6   Casals (A)

177 **NAME CHECK**

1   LIMBS
2   CRIED
3   EVERY
4   TITLE
5   SNAIL
6   AGENT
IRVING BERLIN

178 **RING CYCLE**

1   Einaudi
2   Italian
3   Natural
4   *Leonora*
5   Andante

179 **FAST FORWARD**

CHARD
CHORD

180 **I WAS THERE**

JOHANNES BRAHMS (1833–97)
Borodin died in 1887.
Tchaikovsky died in 1893.
The first Modern Olympics were held in Athens in 1896.

181 **FIVE FIT**

182 **BACK TRACK**

CORSETS
CORNETS

183 **INVISIBLES**

SATIE

184 **MOVIE A TO Z**

CINEMA PARADISO (Ennio Morricone)

185 **COMPOSING**

1	WHISTLE
2	FIDDLER
3	VESPERS
4	TUNEFUL
5	MARIMBA
6	RONDEAU
7	BRITTEN

WISEMAN is formed in the shaded diagonal.

186 **WHAT AM I?**

SCORE

187 **SOUND BITE**

1	Bird / Byrd
2	Handle / Handel
3	Briton / Britten,
4	Back / Bach
5	Vile / Weill

188 **MUSIC BOX**

PODS
OKRA
DRUM
SAME

189 **BACH-WORDS**

LISZT

190 **QUIZ CROSSWORD**

Across
7 Little
9 Operas
10 Diminuendo
11 *Game*
12 Largo
13 Xylophone
15 Tangoes
20 Orchestra
21 Japan
23 *Thor*
24 Recordings
25 Museum
26 Caesar

Down
1 Digital
2 Strings
3 Venus
4 *Monotones*
5 Lengths
6 Harmony
8 Henryk Gorecki
14 Bass drums
16 Orpheus
17 Charles
18 Matinee
19 Vaughan
22 Track

191 **SPIRAL**

1 Melba
2 Banjo
3 Joseph
4 Philip
5 Piano
6 Norman
7 Mandolin
8 Lind
9 Domingo

192 **CIRCLES**

The question mark is the letter R.
Top left: Bayreuth
Top right: Salzburg
Bottom: Lucerne

193 **THE LOST CHORD**

Note G is needed to make AGE.
Saturn is described as the bringer of old age in Holst's *The Planets*.

194 **ALPHA MALE**

BRYN TERFEL

195 **SESTET**

1	Magpie
2	*Eugene*
3	Tenors
4	Samuel
5	Career
6	Madrid
7	Danube
8	Maraca
9	Volume
10	Triple
11	Meters
12	Alfred

196 **TYPO**

KORMA
KORMA should be *NORMA*.

197 **VOWEL PLAY**

London Coliseum

198 **ALPHA MALE**

ALED JONES

199 **SUDO-KEY**

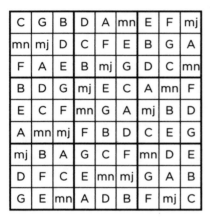

C	G	B	D	A	mn	E	F	mj
mn	mj	D	C	F	E	B	G	A
F	A	E	B	mj	G	D	C	mn
B	D	G	mj	E	C	A	mn	F
E	C	F	mn	G	A	mj	B	D
A	mn	mj	F	B	D	C	E	G
mj	B	A	G	C	F	mn	D	E
D	F	C	E	mn	mj	G	A	B
G	E	mn	A	D	B	F	mj	C

200 **NUMBER SUM**

3 Gymnopédies x The Two Widows = 6

201 **PERFECT FIFTH**

1   Elder
2   Pearl
3   Bream
4   Baker
5   Debut
6   Bugle

202 **A QUIZ FOR CLASSICAL MUSIC EXPERTS**

1   a) Chalumeau
2   c) Teacups on a string
3   a) Wolfgang Amadeus Mozart
4   b) Prompter
5   a) Denis

203 **MISSING VOICES**

THE SEASONS (Haydn)

204 **NINTH SYMPHONY**

a)   CHOPIN
b)   (*The*) *MISSION*
c)   *MY*
SYMPHONIC

205 **FORTUNE TELLER**

Benjamin Britten

206 **METRONOME**

1   Away
2   Gynt
3   Dawn
4   Star
5   Anna
6   Twin

207 **ADDERS**

Maracas

208 **HALF TIME**

1   Peal
2   Also
3   Solo
4   Lost
5   Step

209 **DIMINUENDO**

Benjamin Britten

210 **REARRANGEMENT**

AVID
DIVA

211 **SPLIT PERSONALITY**

THOMAS TALLIS

212 **OCTET**

1   Gershwin (C)
2   *Swan Lake* (C)
3   Ocarinas (C)
4   Dame Kiri (C)
5   Arpeggio (A)
6   *La bohème* (C)
7   Baritone (A)
8   Virtuoso (C)

213 **CYMBALISM**

VIOL
VIVALDI
MANDOLIN
ARNOLD

214 **IN HARMONY**

There are 120 singers: 40 sopranos, 30 altos, 24 tenors and 26 bass.

215 **INVISIBLES**

BYRD

216 **HIDDEN INSTRUMENT**

GONG

217 **VOWEL PLAY**

Don Quixote (Minkus)

218 **PHONOGRAPH**

THE MERRY WIDOW (Lehár)

219 **NATURE NOTES WORD SEARCH**

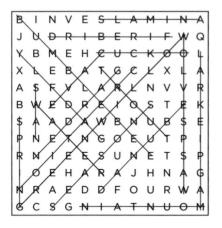

220 **FIVE FIT**

221 ENIGMA VARIATIONS

Across

6	Chorus
7	Lake
9	Caruso
10	Italy
12	Lear
13	Fenby
17	Binge
18	Star
21	Polka
22	Isolde
24	Coda
25	Claude

Down

1	Sonatas
2	Lulu
3	Marimba
4	Pedal
5	Lloyd
8	*Lohengrin*
11	Fly
14	Einaudi
15	Stadium
16	Ark
19	Space
20	*Clock*
23	Oslo

222 FILLERS

ORGAN (MORGANATIC, DISORGANISED, ORGANIC)

223 NUMBER NAMES

CASTANETS = 31
A = 1, N = 2, C = 3, T = 4, S = 5, E = 6

224 RING CYCLE

1	Scarpia
2	Arrange
3	Excerpt
4	Tavener
5	Records

225 CIRCLES

The question mark is the letter N.
Top left: Benedetti
Top right: Kennedy
Bottom: Paganini

226 HEXACHORD

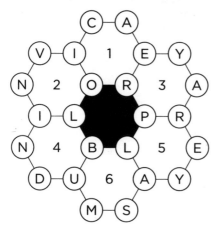

1   *Eroica* (C)
2   Violin (C)
3   Prayer (A)
4   Dublin (A)
5   Player (A)
6   Albums (A)

227 MUSIC BOX

EBBS
BELL
BLUE
SLEW

228 MOVIE A TO Z

DOCTOR ZHIVAGO (Maurice Jarre)

229 **NAME CHECK**

1 LIMITED
2 INITIAL
3 ESCAPED
4 UNHAPPY
5 CHATEAU
6 SPECTRE
7 DILUTED
MICHAEL TIPPETT

230 **PRESTO**

Across
6 Delius
7 Star
9 Yehudi
10 Ad lib
12 Carl
13 Sousa
17 Baker
18 Fine
21 Polka
22 Tuning
24 Tell
25 Scales

Down
1 Allegro
2 Tutu
3 Strauss
4 Trill
5 Melba
8 *Rigoletto*
11 Act
14 Caballé
15 Pianola
16 Key
19 Spain
20 Flute
23 Neck

231 **NUMBER SUM**

1919 + 2 = 1921

232 **FAST FORWARD**

SCARE
SCORE

233 **WHAT AM I?**

NOTE

234 **SPIRAL**

1   Xenakis
2   *Kismet*
3   Smetana
4   Natural
5   Alto
6   Toscanini
7   Nigel
8   Elgar
9   Garden

235 **I WAS THERE**

DMITRI SHOSTAKOVICH (1906–75)
Bartók died in 1945.
Schoenberg died in 1951.
Yuri Gagarin became the first man in space in April 1961.

236 **MISS HERD**

SWEET, HIM and PEEL need to change.
At the after-show refreshments in the church hall, there was much praise for the popular *Nutcracker* suite. The newly divorced soprano, who liked religious music, was in a lengthy discussion about a change of hymn. In a church, all agreed that the peal of the bells, gives an added dimension to the music.

237 **PERFECT FIFTH**

1   Shore
3   Dream
5   Waltz
7   Italy
9   Plain
11   Light

238 **SESTET**

1 Terfel
2 Player
3 Ischia
4 Simple
5 Nuance
6 Stuart
7 Cellos
8 Minuet
9 Chopin
10 Gadfly
11 Gloria
12 Repeat

239 **NINTH SYMPHONY**

a) SUK
b) HARP
c) PETER
PETRUSHKA

240 **BACH-WORDS**

RAVEL

241 **MUSICAL TASTES**

Bass (they have a preference for things with double letters so bass is for them!)

242 **BACK TRACK**

MATCH
MARCH

243 **HALF TIME**

1   Tuba
2   *Bare*
3   Reed
4   Edit
5   Item

244 **SUDO-KEY**

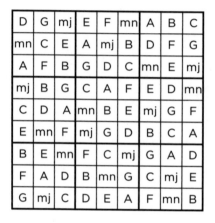

D	G	mj	E	F	mn	A	B	C
mn	C	E	A	mj	B	D	F	G
A	F	B	G	D	C	mn	E	mj
mj	B	G	C	A	F	E	D	mn
C	D	A	mn	B	E	mj	G	F
E	mn	F	mj	G	D	B	C	A
B	E	mn	F	C	mj	G	A	D
F	A	D	B	mn	G	C	mj	E
G	mj	C	D	E	A	F	mn	B

245 **NOTATION**

PACHELBEL
CANON AND GIGUE

246 **FORTUNE TELLER**

Antonin Dvořák

247 **THE LOST CHORD**

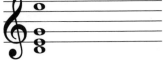

Note D is needed to make EDGE.
Vaughan Williams composed *On Wenlock Edge*.

248 **SPLIT PERSONALITY**

PIERRE BOULEZ

249 **INVISIBLES**

SUK

250 **ALPHA MALE**

FREDDIE DE TOMMASO

251 **REARRANGEMENT**

TASTIER
ARTISTE

252 **TYPO**

THE WING CYCLE
WING should be *RING*.

253 **CIRCLES**

The question mark is the letter A.
Top left: Barenboim
Top right: Ashkenazy
Lower circle: Perahia

254 **ADDERS**

Strings

255 **COMPOSING**

1   VIOLINS
2   PICCOLO
3   REVISED
4   MARACAS
5   POPULAR
6   BALLADS
7   GORECKI
VIVALDI is formed in the shaded diagonal.

256 **METRONOME**

1   Wood
2   Odes
3   Love
4   Oslo
5   Bell
6   Evil

257 **HIDDEN INSTRUMENT**

FIFE

258 **DIMINUENDO**

John Cage

259 WHAT AM I?

CHORD

260 NAME CHECK

1   SHAWL
2   TUTOR
3   AGILE
4   CORFU
HUGO WOLF

261 FILLERS

HORN (QUICKTHORN, THORNBILL, SHORN)

262 GAMERS

Jeff Gold wrote *The Curse of the Grey-Haired Prophet*.
Tom Grey wrote *Escape from the Silver Sentinel*.
Sara Silver wrote *A Goblet Full of Gold*.

263 PHONOGRAPH

THE DREAM OF GERONTIUS (Elgar)

264 OCTET

1   Woodwind (C)
2   Paganini (A)
3   Korngold (C)
4   *Sinfonia* (A)
5   Mandolin (C)
6   Sullivan (C)
7   Pastoral (A)
8   Clarinet (A)

265 **FIVE FIT**

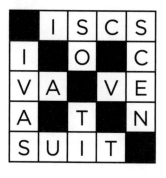

266 **RING CYCLE**

1   Haitink
2   *Karelia*
3   Applaud
4   Dancers
5   Seventh

267 **CYMBALISM**

TUBA
STRAUSS
SATURN
URANUS

268 **NUMBER NAMES**

ORATORIO = 29
D = 1, O = 2, I = 3, T = 4, R = 5, A = 6

269 **MUSIC BOX**

OPUS
PIPE
UPON
SEND

270 FAST FORWARD

PINES
PIPES

271 SPIRAL

1 Gabetta
2 Tango
3 Goodall
4 Allegro
5 Rodrigo
6 Gobbi
7 Binge
8 Gershwin

272 QUICK QUOTE

1 Pianist
2 Musical
3 Chamber
4 Perform
5 Filming
6 Angeles
7 Houston
Quotation: *being the traffic cop*

273 I WAS THERE

FRANZ SCHUBERT (1797–1828)
Haydn died in 1809.
Mozart died in 1791.
The brothers Grimm produced their first volume of fairy tales in 1812.

274 BACK TRACK

AYR
AIR

275 **MOVIE A TO Z**

SAVING PRIVATE RYAN (John Williams)

276 **QUIZ CROSSWORD**

Across

7   Caruso
9   Evelyn
10   Major scale
11   Eric
12   *Brief*
13   Edwardian
15   Fiddler
20   Morecambe
21   Venue
23   Four
24   Instrument
25   Robert
26   Daniel

Down

1   Macabre
2   Tutored
3   Holst
4   Serenades
5   Legends
6   Lyrical
8   Claude Debussy
14   Finalists
16   *Solomon*
17   Ferrier
18   Germany
19   *Quintet*
22   *Pride*

277 **SESTET**

1   Ballet
2   Edward
3   Enrico
4   Bridge
5   Ascend
6   Porter
7   *Garden*
8   Presto
9   Fiddle
10   Italia
11   Studio
12   Leader

278 **BACH-WORDS**

SATIE

279 **ALPHA MALE**

LUCIANO PAVAROTTI

280 **PHONOGRAPH**

THE BLUE DANUBE (Strauss)

281 **THE LOST CHORD**

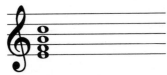

Note C is needed to make CAFE.
Café Society described creative gatherings at fashionable locations.

282 **NINTH SYMPHONY**

a)   THEME
b)   *AIDA*
c)   KOKO
THE MIKADO

283 **SUDO-KEY**

D	mn	C	F	E	G	A	B	mj
B	mj	E	mn	A	D	G	C	F
F	G	A	B	C	mj	E	D	mn
C	D	B	mj	G	F	mn	A	E
G	E	mj	C	mn	A	D	F	B
A	F	mn	D	B	E	C	mj	G
E	B	D	A	F	mn	mj	G	C
mn	A	F	G	mj	C	B	E	D
mj	C	G	E	D	B	F	mn	A

284 **VOWEL PLAY**

Bolshoi Theatre

285 **HEXACHORD**

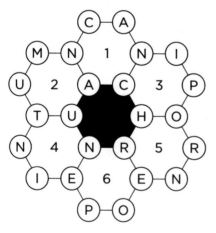

1	Can can (C)
2	Autumn (C)
3	Chopin (A)
4	In tune (C)
5	Horner (C)
6	Reopen (C)

286 **PERFECT FIFTH**

1	Baton
3	*Tosca*
5	Score
7	Trout
9	Lutes
11	Lehár

287 **FORTUNE TELLER**

Aaron Copland

288 **REARRANGEMENT**

ARTICLE
RECITAL

289 **CIRCLES**

The question mark is the letter M.
Top left: Oramo
Top right: Dudamel
Bottom: Marriner

290 **MISSING VOICES**

STABAT MATER (Pergolesi)

291 **HALF TIME**

1	Capo
2	Poem
3	Emma
4	Maid
5	Idea

292 **NUMBER SUM**

Symphony No. 9 x 5 lines on a stave = 45

293 **ADDERS**

Reprise

294 **SEATING PLAN**

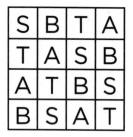

295 **NOTATION**

DELIBES
COPPÉLIA

296 **NAME CHECK**

1   THOUGHT
2   CORDIAL
3   SOLUBLE
4   BRAMBLE
5   GONDOLA
6   TIDINGS
7   BLOSSOM
ORLANDO GIBBONS

297 'JERUSALEM' WORD SEARCH

298 **METRONOME**

1 *Asia*
2 Cave
3 Kiev
4 Jess
5 Ives
6 Hebe

299 **SPLIT PERSONALITY**

GUSTAV MAHLER

300 **INVISIBLES**

BRAHMS

301 **HIDDEN INSTRUMENT**

SITAR

302 **VOWEL PLAY**

Romeo and Juliet (Prokofiev)

303 **CYMBALISM**

OBOE
BOLERO
BARBER
TREBLE

304 **OCTET**

1 *Falstaff* (C)
2 Lang Lang (C)
3 Soloists (C)
4 Operetta (A)
5 Sopranos (A)
6 Organist (C)
7 Grainger (A)
8 Mascagni (A)

305 **ENIGMA VARIATIONS**

Across
6 Callas
7 Gala
9 Bridge
10 Label
12 *Aida*
13 Pitch
17 Tango
18 *Così*
21 Holst
22 Artist
24 Time
25 Gloria

Down
1 Florida
2 Band
3 Wallace
4 Samba
5 Cello
8 *Leningrad*
11 Fan
14 Ragtime
15 Consort
16 Air
19 Choir
20 Flats
23 Tell

306 **NUMBER NAMES**

TALLIS = 20
L = 1, E = 2, A = 3, T = 4, S = 5, I = 6

307 **TYPO**

THE DANCE OF THE SUGAR GLUM FAIRY
GLUM should be *PLUM.*

308 **RING CYCLE**

1   Ireland
2   Descant
3   Touring
4   Gardner
5   Rossini

309 **PHONOGRAPH**

TRUMPET VOLUNTARY (Stanley)

310 **I WAS THERE**

ENGELBERT HUMPERDINCK (1854–1921)
Hubert Parry died in 1918.
Rimsky-Korsakov died in 1908.
Alcock and Brown flew across the Atlantic in 1919.

311 **MISSING VOICES**

ST CECILIA MASS (Gounod)

312 **FIVE FIT**

313 **FILLERS**

CUE (EVACUEE, RESCUED, BARBECUE)

314 **PRESTO**

Across

6	Lieder
7	Kiwi
9	Rattle
10	Pears
12	Eric
13	Heath
17	*Hours*
18	Hero
21	Oramo
22	Alagna
24	Brio
25	Bartok

Down

1	Xenakis
2	West
3	Tippett
4	Milan
5	*Faust*
8	Rehearsal
11	*Sea*
14	Borodin
15	Bennett
16	*Joy*
19	Solti
20	Samba
23	Adam

315 **WHAT AM I?**

STAVE

316 **FAST FORWARD**

PINCH
PITCH

317 **MOVIE A TO Z**

THE PINK PANTHER (Henry Mancini)

318 **DIMINUENDO**

Franz Lehár

319 **TRANSPOSED**

BANJO
Each letter in FERNS moves back four places in alphabetical order to produce BANJO.

320 **MUSIC BOX**

LUTE
USER
TEAR
ERRS

321 **BACH-WORDS**

ELGAR

322 **HEXACHORD**

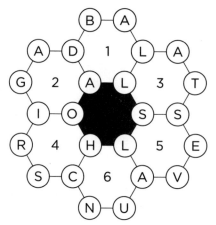

1   Ballad (C)
2   Adagio (A)
3   Stalls (A)
4   Choirs (A)
5   Slaves (A)
6   Launch (C)

323 **BACK TO SCHOOL MUSIC QUIZ**

1   b) A couple's dance
2   a) A brass instrument, like a baby trumpet
3   c) Tambourine
4   b) If someone who has never loved before swears an oath of undying love
5   c) Für Elise

324 **BACK TRACK**

PETAL
PEDAL

325 **SPIRAL**

1 Piccolo
2 Lott
3 *Turandot*
4 Otter
5 Terfyl
6 Lyricist
7 Strauss
8 *Sea*

326 **NINTH SYMPHONY**

a) SINGER
b) TUNE
c) SITAR
SIGNATURE

327 **FORTUNE TELLER**

Alexander Borodin

328 **PERFECT FIFTH**

1   Minor
3   Sousa
5   Psalm
7   Flute
9   Steps
11 April

329 **THE LOST CHORD**

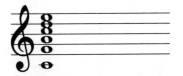

Note A is needed to make *FAÇADE*.
Walton produced the music to accompany these poems by Edith Sitwell.

330 **REARRANGEMENT**

ROASTING
ORGANIST

331 **NUMBER NAMES**

FIDELIO = 22
I = 1, L = 2, E = 3, D = 4, O = 5, F = 6

332 **MISSING VOICES**

SAMSON (Handel)

333 **ADDERS**

Cantata

334 **THE CLASSICAL MUSICAL PUB QUIZ**

1   c) The Slave of Duty
2   b) Brahms
3   c) India
4   d) Hovercraft
5   a) 4

335 **NAME CHECK**

1   OMAHA
2   TYRES
3   FROST
4   DAISY
MYRA HESS

336 ALPHA MALE

ENRICO CARUSO

337 METRONOME

1 Fine
2 Kent
3 Anon
4 Eton
5 *Into*
6 *Post*

338 SPLIT PERSONALITY

FRANCIS POULENC

339 SUDO-KEY

mn	B	A	C	F	mj	G	E	D
E	mj	C	B	D	G	A	mn	F
F	G	D	E	mn	A	C	mj	B
G	E	B	F	mj	mn	D	C	A
A	F	mj	D	C	B	E	G	mn
D	C	mn	G	A	E	B	F	mj
mj	D	G	mn	B	C	F	A	E
B	mn	E	A	G	F	mj	D	C
C	A	F	mj	E	D	mn	B	G

340 FILLERS

REED (BREEDING, GREEDINESS, FREEDOM)

341 **FORTUNE TELLER**

Samuel Barber

342 **ANOTHER QUIZ FOR CLASSICAL MUSIC EXPERTS**

1   a) Dorian
2   c) B flat major
3   c) Appendiabiti
4   a) Two and a half
5   a) Toccata

343 **FILLERS**

BAR (BARRISTER, GABARDINE, EMBARRASS)

344 **THE CLASSICAL MUSIC REVISION QUIZ**

1   d) Eroica
2   c) Saint-Saëns
3   b) Dogfish
4   a) The Bat
5   c) 30 days

345 **ADDERS**

Whistle

346 **HEXACHORD**

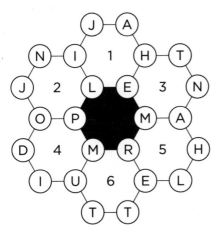

1   Elijah (C)
2   Joplin (A)
3   Anthem (A)
4   Podium (A)
5   Mahler (C)
6   Mutter (A)

347 **HIDDEN INSTRUMENT**

BANJO

348 **FAST FORWARD**

DRAMS
DRUMS

349 **SESTET**

1 Russia
2 *Otello*
3 Cradle
4 Prague
5 Throat
6 Create
7 Guitar
8 Arthur
9 Adagio
10 Damsel
11 *Salome*
12 Kettle

350 **THE SINGING OPTOMETRIST**

It's a feature of the shape of the letters that links all the names. All the individual letters have horizontal symmetry: the top half mirrors the lower half. By applying this eye chart approach Seymore severely limits the roles he can audition for. The logic *is* reasoned and consistent – we didn't say it was sensible!

351 **BACK TRACK**

CONVERT
CONCERT

352 **A BONUS MUSIC TRIVIA QUIZ**

1 a) A bumblebee
2 c) *The Barber of Seville* (Rossini)
3 c) Haydn
4 a) The first African American to win a Pulitzer Prize for Music
5 a) Schoenberg

353 **MOVIE A TO Z**

CHARIOTS OF FIRE (Vangelis)

354 **DIMINUENDO**

Felix Mendelssohn

355 **I WAS THERE**

RALPH VAUGHAN WILLIAMS (1872-1958)
Sergei Prokofiev died in March 1953.
Kurt Weill died in 1950.
The coronation of Queen Elizabeth II took place in June 1953.

356 **MISSING VOICES**

EXSULTATE, JUBILATE (Mozart)

357 **OCTET**

1   Sibelius (C)
2   Minstrel (C)
3   Overture (C)
4   Arvo Pärt (C)
5   Bruckner (C)
6   Concerto (A)
7   Messiaen (A)
8   Trumpets (A)

358 **HEXACHORD**

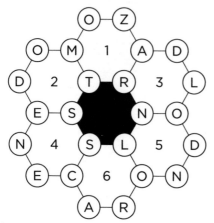

1   Mozart (C)
2   Modest (A)
3   Arnold (A)
4   Scenes (C)
5   London (A)
6   Carols (A)

359 **QUICK QUOTE**

1   Germany
2   Italian
3   *Anthems*
4   Fanfare
5   Solomon
6   Messiah
7   Trumpet
Quotation: *[a grand whim] for posterity to laugh at.*

360 **NOTATION**

HANDEL
SARABANDE

361 CYMBALISM

CELLO
REEL
CORELLI
LYRIC

362 WHAT AM I?

CAROL

363 NUMBER SUM

9 symphonies x 12 days of Christmas = 108

364 GUESS THE CHRISTMAS CAROL

1   'O Holy Night'
2   'The Twelve Days of Christmas'
3   'Little Drummer Boy'
4   'The First Noël'
5   'Carol of the Bells'
6   'Jesus Christ the Apple Tree'
7   'Past Three O'Clock'
8   'Hark! The Herald Angels Sing'
9   'See Amid the Winter's Snow'
10   'Joy to the World'
11   'I Saw Three Ships'
12   'Silent Night'

365 **CHRISTMAS CAROL LYRICS QUIZ**

1   a) On the Feast of Stephen

2   c) Was to certain poor shepherds in fields as they lay

3   b) And pleasure dearly I have bought

4   d) Bearing gifts we traverse afar

5   c) For Thee I yearn away

6   a) For to preserve this day

7   c) Who is God and Lord of all

8   a) The little Lord Jesus asleep on the hay

9   b) Their watch of wondering love

10   a) Lo, He abhors not the Virgin's womb

11   c) Nor earth sustain

NOTES

Also available

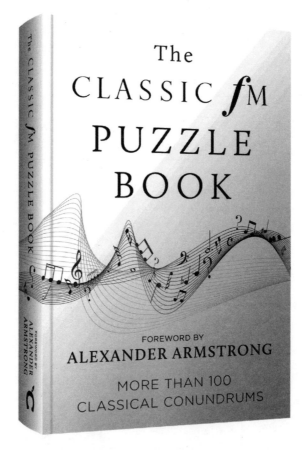

Racism at Work

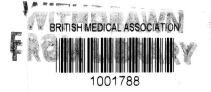